# Harvest of Flavor

# A Culinary Exploration of Living

## By

## Guadalupe R. Cambridge

# Harvest of Flavor

**EEL PIE.**

*Ingredients.*—1 lb. of eels, a little chopped parsley, 1 shalot, grated nutmeg, pepper and salt to taste, the juice of ½ a lemon, small quantity of forcemeat, ¼ pint of Béchamel; puff paste. *Mode.*—Skin and wash the eels, cut them in pieces 2 inches long, and line the bottom of the pie-dish with forcemeat. Put in the eels, and sprinkle them with the parsley, shalots, nutmeg, seasoning, and lemon-juice, and cover with puff paste. Bake for 1 hour, or rather more; make the Béchamel hot, and pour it into the pie. *Time.*—Rather more than 1 hour. *Seasonable* from August to March.

**EEL SOUP.**

*Ingredients.*—3 lbs. of eels, 1 onion, 2 oz. of butter, 3 blades of mace, 1 bunch of sweet herbs, ¼ oz. of peppercorns, salt to taste, 2 tablespoonfuls of flour, ¼ pint of cream, 2 quarts of water. *Mode.*—Wash the eels, cut them into thin slices, and put them into the stewpan with the butter; let them simmer for a few minutes, then pour the water to them, and add the onion, cut in thin slices, the herbs, mace, and seasoning. Simmer till the eels are tender, but do not break the fish. Take them out carefully, mix the flour smoothly to a batter with the cream, bring it to a boil, pour over the eels, and serve. *Time.*—1 hour or rather more. *Average cost,* 10*d.* per quart. *Seasonable* from June to March. *Sufficient* for 8 persons.

*Note.*—This soup may be flavoured differently by omitting the cream, and adding a little ketchup or Harvey's sauce.

**EELS, Boiled.**

*Ingredients.*—4 small eels, sufficient water to cover them; a large bunch of parsley. *Mode.*—Choose small eels for boiling; put them into a stewpan with the parsley, and just sufficient water to cover them; simmer till tender. Take them out, pour a little parsley and butter over them, and serve some in a tureen. *Time.*—½ hour. *Average cost,* 6d. per lb. *Seasonable* from June to March. *Sufficient* for 4 persons.

## EEL,Collar ed.

*Ingredients.*—1 large eel; pepper and salt to taste; 2 blades of mace, 2 cloves, a little allspice very finely pounded, 6 leaves of sage, and a small bunch of herbs minced very small. *Mode.*—Bone the eel and skin it; split it, and sprinkle it over with the ingredients, taking care that the spices are very finely pounded, and the herbs chopped very small. Roll it up and bind with a broad piece of tape, and boil it in water, mixed with a little salt and vinegar, till tender. It may either be served whole or cut in slices; and when cold, the eel should be kept in the liquor it was boiled in, but with a little more vinegar put to it. *Time.*—2 hours. *Averagecost* , 6d. per lb. *Seasonable* from August to March.

## EELS,Fried.

*Ingredients.*—1 lb. of eels, 1 egg, a few bread-crumbs, hot lard. *Mode.*—Wash the eels, cut them into pieces 3 inches long, trim and wipe them very dry; dredge with flour, rub them over with egg, and cover with bread-crumbs; fry a nice brown in hot lard. If the eels are small, curl them round, instead of cutting them up. Garnish with fried parsley. *Time.*—20 minutes or rather less. *Averagecost* , 6d. per lb. *Seasonable* from June to March.

## EELS,enMatelote.

*Ingredients.*—5 or 6 young onions, a few mushrooms, when obtainable; salt, pepper, and nutmeg to taste; 1 laurel leaf, ½ pint of port wine, ½ pint of medium stock, butter and flour to thicken; 2 lbs. of eels. *Mode.*—Rub the stewpan with butter, dredge in a little flour, add the onions cut very small, slightly brown them, and put in all the other ingredients. Wash, and cut up the eels into pieces 3 inches long; put them in the stewpan, and simmer for ½ hour. Make round the dish a border of croûtons, or pieces of toasted bread; arrange the eels in a pyramid in the centre, and pour over the sauce. Serve very hot. *Time.*—¾ hour. *Average cost*, 1*s.* 9*d.* for this quantity. *Seasonable* from August to March. *Sufficient* for 5 or 6 persons.

## EELS, Stewed.

*Ingredients.*—2 lbs. of eels, 1 pint of rich strong stock, 1 onion, 3 cloves, a piece of lemon-peel, 1 glass of port or Madeira, 3 tablespoonfuls of cream; thickening of flour; cayenne and lemon-juice to taste. *Mode.*—Wash and skin the eels, and cut them into pieces about 3 inches long; pepper and salt them, and lay them in a stewpan; pour over the stock, add the onion stuck with cloves, the lemon-peel, and the wine. Stew gently for ½ hour, or rather more, and lift them carefully on a dish, which keep hot. Strain the gravy, stir the cream, sufficient flour to thicken; mix altogether, boil for 2 minutes, and add the cayenne and lemon-juice; pour over the eels and serve. *Time.*—¾ hour. *Average cost* for this quantity, 2*s.* 3*d.* *Seasonable* from June to March. *Sufficient* for 5 or 6 persons.

## EELS, Stewed.

*Ingredients.*—2 lbs. of middling-sized eels, 1 pint of medium stock, ¼ pint of port wine; salt, cayenne, and mace to taste; 1 teaspoonful of essence of anchovy, the juice of ½ a lemon. *Mode.*—Skin, wash, and clean the eels, thoroughly; cut them into pieces 3 inches long, and put them into strong salt and water for 1 hour; dry them well with a cloth, and fry them brown. Put the stock on with the heads and tails of the eels, and simmer for ½ hour; strain it, and add all the other ingredients. Put in the eels, and stew gently for ½ hour, when serve. *Time.*—2 hours. *Average cost*, 1*s.* 9*d.* *Seasonable* from June to March. *Sufficient* for 5 or 6 persons.

## EELS, à la Tartare.

*Ingredients.*—2 lbs. of eels, 1 carrot, 1 onion, a little flour, 1 glass of sherry; salt, pepper, and nutmeg to taste; bread-crumbs, 1 egg, 2 tablespoonfuls of vinegar. *Mode.*—Rub the butter on the bottom of the stewpan; cut up the carrot and onion, and stir them over the fire for 5 minutes; dredge in a little flour, add the wine and seasoning, and boil for ½ an hour. Skin and wash the eels, cut them into pieces, put them to the other ingredients, and simmer till tender. When they are done, take them out, let them get cold, cover them with egg and bread-crumbs, and fry them of a nice brown. Put them on a dish, pour sauce piquante over, and serve them hot. *Time.*—1½ hour. *Averagecost* , 1*s.* 8*d.*, exclusive of the sauce piquante. *Seasonable* from August to March. *Sufficient* for 5 or 6 persons.

## EGGS.

There is only one opinion as to the nutritive properties of eggs, although the qualities of those belonging to different birds vary somewhat. Those of the common hen are most esteemed as delicate food, particularly when "new-laid." The quality of eggs depends much upon the food given to the hen. Eggs in general are considered most easily digestible when little subjected to the art of cookery. The lightest way of dressing them is by poaching, which is effected by putting them for a minute or two into brisk boiling water: this coagulates the external white, without doing the inner part too much. Eggs are much better when new-laid than a day or two afterwards. The usual time allotted for boiling eggs in the shell is 3 to 3¾ minutes: less time than that in boiling water will not be sufficient to solidify the white, and more will make the yolk hard and less digestible: it is very difficult to *guess* accurately as to the time. Great care should be employed in putting them into the water, to prevent cracking the shell, which inevitably causes a portion of the white to exude, and lets water into the egg. For the purpose of placing eggs in water, always choose a *large* spoon in preference to a small one. Eggs are often beaten up raw in nutritive beverages.

The eggs of the *turkey* are almost as mild as those of the hen; the egg of the *goose* is large, but well-tasted. *Ducks' eggs* have a rich flavour; the albumen is slightly transparent, or bluish, when set or coagulated by boiling, which requires less time than hens' eggs. *Guinea-fowl eggs* are smaller and more delicate than those of the hen. Eggs of *wild fowl* are generally coloured, often spotted; and the taste generally partakes somewhat of the bird they belong to. Those of land birds that are eaten, as the *plover, lapwing, ruff*, &c., are in general much esteemed; but those of *sea-fowl* have, more or less, a strong fishy taste. The eggs of the *turtle* are very numerous: they consist of yolk only, without shell, and are delicious.

When fresh eggs are dropped into a vessel *full* of boiling water, they crack, because the eggs being well filled, the shells give way to the efforts of the interior fluids, dilated by heat. If the volume of hot water be small, the shells do not crack, because its temperature is reduced by the eggs before the interior dilation can take place. Stale eggs, again, do not crack because the air inside is easily compressed.

## EGGBALLS, for Soups and made Dishes.

*Ingredients.*—8 eggs, a little flour; seasoning to taste of salt. *Mode.*—Boil 6 eggs for 20 minutes, strip off the shells, take the yolks and pound them in a mortar. Beat the yolks of the 2 uncooked eggs; add them, with a little flour and salt, to those pounded; mix all well together, and roll into balls. Boil them before they are put into the soup or other dish they may be intended for.

## EGGSAUCE, for Salt Fish.

*Ingredients.*—4 eggs, ½ pint of melted butter, when liked, a very little lemon-juice. *Mode.*—Boil the eggs until quite hard, which will be in about 20 minutes, and put them into cold water for ½ hour. Strip off the shells, chop the eggs into small pieces, not, however, too fine. Make the melted butter very smooth, and, when boiling, stir in the eggs, and serve very hot. Lemon-juice may be added at pleasure. *Time.*—20 minutes to boil the eggs. *Average cost*, 8*d*. *Sufficient.*—This quantity for 3 or 4 lbs. of fish.

*Note.*—When a thicker sauce is required, use one or two more eggs to the same quantity of melted butter.

## EGGSOUP.

*Ingredients.*—A tablespoonful of flour, 4 eggs, 2 small blades of finely-pounded mace, 2 quarts of stock. *Mode.*—Beat up the flour smoothly in a teaspoonful of cold stock, and put in the eggs; throw them into boiling stock, stirring all the time. Simmer for ¼ of an hour. Season and serve with a French roll in the tureen or fried sippets of bread. *Time.*—½ an hour. *Average cost*, 11*d*. per quart. *Seasonable* all the year. *Sufficient* for 8 persons.

# EGGWINE.

*Ingredients.*—1 egg, 1 tablespoonful and ½ glass of cold water, 1 glass of sherry, sugar and grated nutmeg to taste. *Mode.*—Beat the egg, mixing with it a tablespoonful of cold water; make the wine-and-water hot, but not boiling; pour it on the egg, stirring all the time. Add sufficient lump sugar to sweeten the mixture, and a little grated nutmeg; put all into a very clean saucepan, set it on a gentle fire, and stir the contents one way until they thicken, but *do not allow them to boil*. Serve in a glass with sippets of toasted bread or plain crisp biscuits. When the egg is not warmed, the mixture will be found easier of digestion, but it is not so pleasant a drink. *Sufficient* for 1 person.

## EGGS, to Boil for Breakfast, Salads, &c.

Eggs for boiling cannot be too fresh, or boiled too soon after they are laid; but rather a longer time should be allowed for boiling a new-laid egg than for one that is three or four days old. Have ready a saucepan of boiling water; put the eggs into it gently with a spoon, letting the spoon touch the bottom of the saucepan before it is withdrawn, that the egg may not fall, and consequently crack. For those who like eggs lightly boiled, 3 minutes will be found sufficient; 3¾ to 4 minutes will be ample time to set the white nicely; and, if liked hard, 6 to 7 minutes will not be found too long. Should the eggs be unusually large, as those of black Spanish fowls sometimes are, allow an extra ½ minute for them. Eggs for salads should be boiled from 10 minutes to ¼ hour, and should be placed in a basin of cold water for a few minutes; they should then be rolled on the table with the hand, and the shell will peel off easily. *Time.*—To boil eggs lightly, for invalids or children, 3 minutes; to boil eggs to suit the generality of tastes, 3¾ to 4 minutes; to boil eggs hard, 6 to 7 minutes; for salads, 10 to 15 minutes.

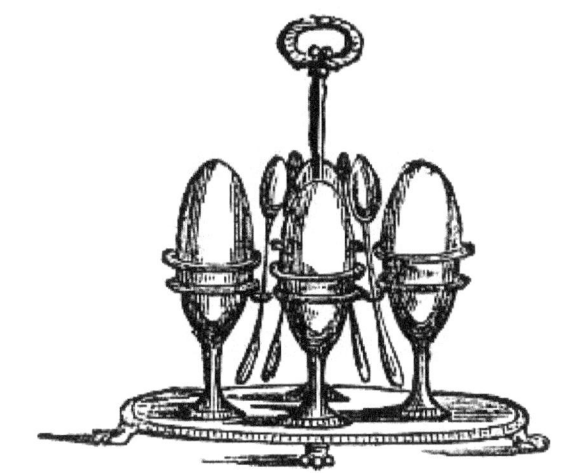

EGG-STAND FOR THE BREAKFAST-TABLE.

## EGGS, Buttered.

*Ingredients.*—4 new-laid eggs, 2 oz. of butter. *Mode.*—Procure the eggs new-laid if possible; break them into a basin, and beat them well; put the butter into another basin, which place in boiling water, and stir till the butter is melted. Pour that and the eggs into a lined saucepan; hold it over a gentle fire, and, as the mixture begins to warm, pour it two or three times into the basin, and back again, that the two ingredients may be well incorporated. Keep stirring the eggs and butter one way until they are hot, *without boiling*, and serve on hot buttered toast. If the mixture is allowed to boil, it will curdle, and so be entirely spoiled. *Time.*—About 5 minutes to make the eggs hot. *Average cost*, 7d. *Sufficient.*—Allow a slice to each person. *Seasonable* at any time.

## EGGS, to Choose.

In choosing eggs, apply the tongue to the large end of the egg, and, if it feels warm, it is new, and may be relied on as a fresh egg. Another mode of ascertaining their freshness is to hold them before a lighted candle or to the light, and, if the egg looks clear, it will be tolerably good; if thick, it is stale; and if there is a black spot attached to the shell, it is worthless. No egg should be used for culinary purposes with the slightest taint in it, as it will render perfectly useless those with which it has been mixed. Eggs that are purchased, and that cannot be relied on, should always be broken in a cup, and then put into a basin: by this means stale or bad eggs may be easily rejected, without wasting the others.

## EGGS, Ducks'.

Ducks' eggs are usually so strongly flavoured that, plainly boiled, they are not good for eating; they answer, however, very well for various culinary preparations where eggs are required; such as custards, &c. &c. Being so large and highly-flavoured, 1 duck's egg will go as far as 2 small hen's eggs, besides making whatever they are mixed with exceedingly rich. They also are admirable when used in puddings.

## EGGS, Fried.

*Ingredients.*—4 eggs, ¼ lb. of lard, butter or clarified dripping. *Mode.*—Place a delicately-clean frying-pan over a gentle fire; put in the fat, and allow it to come to the boiling-point. Break the eggs into cups, slip them into the boiling fat, and let them remain until the whites are delicately set; and, whilst they are frying, ladle a little of the fat over them. Take them up with a slice, drain them for a minute from their greasy moisture, trim them neatly, and serve on slices of fried bacon or ham; or the eggs may be placed in the middle of the dish, with the bacon put round as a garnish. *Time.*—2 to 3 minutes. *Averagecost*, 1*d.* each; 2*d.* when scarce. *Sufficient* for 2 persons. *Seasonable* at any time.

**FRIED EGGS ON BACON.**

## EGGS à la Maître d'Hôtel.

*Ingredients.*—¼ lb. of fresh butter, 1 tablespoonful of flour, ½ pint of milk, pepper and salt to taste, 1 tablespoonful of minced parsley, the juice of ½ lemon, 6 eggs. *Mode.*—Put the flour and half the butter into a stewpan; stir them over the fire until the mixture thickens; pour in the milk, which should be boiling; add a seasoning of pepper and salt, and simmer the whole for 5 minutes. Put the remainder of the butter into the sauce, and add the minced parsley; then boil the eggs hard, strip off the shell, cut the eggs into quarters, and put them on a dish. Bring the sauce to the boiling-point, add the lemon-juice, pour over the eggs and serve. *Time.*—5 minutes to boil the sauce; the eggs, 10 to 15 minutes. *Average cost*, 1s. *Sufficient* for 4 or 5 persons. *Seasonable* at any time.

## EGGS, to Pickle.

*Ingredients.*—16 eggs, 1 quart of vinegar, ½ oz. of black pepper, ½ oz. of Jamaica pepper, ½ oz. of ginger. *Mode.*—Boil the eggs for 12 minutes, then dip them into cold water, and take off the shells. Put the vinegar, with the pepper and ginger, into a stewpan, and let it simmer for 10 minutes. Now place the eggs in a jar, pour over them the vinegar, &c., boiling hot, and, when cold, tie them down with bladder to exclude the air. This pickle will be ready for use in a month. *Average cost*, for this quantity, 1s. 9d. *Seasonable.*—This should be made about Easter, as at this time eggs are plentiful and cheap. A store of pickled eggs will be found very useful and ornamental in serving with many first and second course dishes.

## EGGS AU PLAT, or AU MIROIR, served on the Dish in which they are Cooked.

*Ingredients.*—4 eggs, 1 oz. of butter, pepper and salt to taste. *Mode.*—Butter a dish rather thickly with good fresh butter; melt it, break the eggs into it the same as for poaching, sprinkle them with white pepper and fine salt, and put the remainder of the butter, cut into very small pieces, on the top of them. Put the dish on a hot plate, or in the oven, or before the fire, and let it remain until the whites become set, but not hard, when serve immediately, placing the dish they were cooked in on another. To hasten the cooking of the eggs, a salamander may be held over them for a minute; but great care must be taken that they are not too much done. This is an exceedingly nice dish, and one very easily prepared for breakfast. *Time.*—3 minutes. *Average cost,* 5d. *Sufficient* for 2 persons. *Seasonable* at any time.

## EGGS, Plovers'.

Plovers' eggs are usually served boiled hard, and sent to table in a napkin, either hot or cold; they may also be shelled, and served the same as eggs à la Tripe, with a good Béchamel sauce, or brown gravy, poured over them. They are also used for decorating salads, the beautiful colour of the white being generally so much admired.

## EGGS, Poached.

*Ingredients.*—Eggs, water. To every pint of water allow 1 tablespoonful of vinegar. *Mode.*—Eggs for poaching should be perfectly fresh, but not quite new-laid; those that are about 36 hours old are the best for the purpose. If quite new-laid, the white is so milky it is almost impossible to set it; and, on the other hand, if the egg be at all stale, it is equally difficult to poach it nicely. Strain some boiling water into a deep clean frying-pan; break the egg into a cup without damaging the yolk, and, when the water boils, remove the pan to the side of the fire, and gently slip the egg into it. Place the pan over a gentle fire, and keep the water simmering until the white looks nicely set, when the egg is ready. Take it up gently with a slice, cut away the ragged edges of the white, and serve either on toasted bread or on slices of ham or bacon, or on spinach, &c. A poached egg should not be overdone, as its appearance and taste will be quite spoiled if the yolk be allowed to harden. When the egg is slipped into the water, the white should be gathered together, to keep it a little in form, or the cup should be turned over it for ½ minute. To poach an egg to perfection is rather a difficult operation; so, for inexperienced cooks, a tin egg-poacher may be purchased, which greatly facilitates this manner of dressing eggs. Our illustration clearly shows what it is: it consists of a tin plate with a handle, with a space for three perforated cups. An egg should be broken into each cup, and the machine then placed in a stewpan of boiling water, which has been previously strained. When the whites of the eggs appear set, they are done, and should then be carefully slipped on to the toast or spinach, or with whatever they are served. In poaching eggs in a frying-pan, never do more than four at a time; and, when a little vinegar is liked mixed with the water in which the eggs are done, use the above proportion. *Time.*—2½ to 3½ minutes, according to the size of the egg. *Sufficient.*—Allow 2 eggs to each person. *Seasonable* at any time, but less plentiful in winter.

**EGGS POACHED ON TOAST.**

**TIN EGG-POACHER.**

## EGGS, Poached, with Cream.

*Ingredients.*—1 pint of water, 1 teaspoonful of salt, 4 teaspoonfuls of vinegar, 4 fresh eggs, ½ gill of cream, salt, pepper, and pounded sugar to taste, 1 oz. of butter. *Mode.*—Put the water, vinegar, and salt into a frying-pan, and break each egg into a separate cup; bring the water, &c., to boil, and slip the eggs gently into it without breaking the yolks. Simmer them from 3 to 4 minutes, but not longer, and, with a slice, lift them out on to a hot dish, and trim the edges. Empty the pan of its contents, put in the cream, add a seasoning to taste of pepper, salt, and pounded sugar; bring the whole to the boiling-point; then add the butter, broken into small pieces; toss the pan round and round till the butter is melted; pour it over the eggs, and serve. To insure the eggs not being spoiled whilst the cream, &c. is preparing, it is a good plan to warm the cream with the butter, &c. before the eggs are poached, so that it may be poured over them immediately after they are dished. *Time.*—3 to 4 minutes to poach the eggs, 5 minutes to warm the cream. *Average cost* for the above quantity, 9d. *Sufficient* for 2 persons. *Seasonable* at any time.

## EGGS, Scotch.

*Ingredients.*—6 eggs, 6 tablespoonfuls of forcemeat, hot lard, ½ pint of good brown gravy. *Mode.*—Boil the eggs for 10 minutes; strip them from the shells, and cover them with forcemeat, or substitute pounded anchovies for the ham. Fry the eggs a nice brown in boiling lard, drain them before the fire from their greasy moisture, dish them, and pour round from ¼ to ½ pint of good brown gravy. To enhance the appearance of the eggs, they may be rolled in beaten egg and sprinkled with bread-crumbs; but this is scarcely necessary if they are carefully fried. The flavour of the ham or the anchovy in the forcemeat must preponderate, as it should be very relishing. *Time.*—10 minutes to boil the eggs, 5 to 7 minutes to fry them. *Average cost*, 1s. 4d. *Sufficient* for 3 or 4 persons. *Seasonable* at any time.

## EGGS, Snow, or Œufs à la Neige (a very pretty Supper Dish).

*Ingredients.*—4 eggs, ¾ pint of milk, pounded sugar to taste, flavouring of vanilla, lemon-rind, or orange-flower water. *Mode.*—Put the milk into a saucepan with sufficient sugar to sweeten it nicely, and the rind of ½ lemon. Let this steep by the side of the fire for ½ hour, when take out the peel; separate the whites from the yolks of the eggs, and whisk the former to a perfectly stiff froth, or until there is no liquid remaining; bring the milk to the boiling-point, drop in the snow a tablespoonful at a time, and keep turning the eggs until sufficiently cooked. Then place them on a glass dish, beat up the yolks of the eggs, stir to them the milk, add a little more sugar, and strain this mixture into a jug; place the jug in a saucepan of boiling water, and stir it one way until the mixture thickens, but do not allow it to boil, or it will curdle. Pour this custard over the eggs, when they should rise to the surface. They make an exceedingly pretty addition to a supper, and should be put in a cold place after being made. When they are flavoured with vanilla or orange-flowered water, it is not necessary to steep the milk. A few drops of the essence of either may be poured into the milk just before the whites are poached. In making the custard, a little more flavouring and sugar should always be added. *Time.*—About 2 minutes to poach the whites; 8 minutes to stir the custard. *Average cost*, 8*d*. *Sufficient* for 4 or 5 persons. *Seasonable* at any time.

## EGGS, to keep Fresh for several Weeks.

Have ready a large saucepan, capable of holding 3 or 4 quarts, full of boiling water. Put the eggs into a cabbage-net, say 20 at a time, and hold them in the water (which must be kept boiling) *for* 20 *seconds*. Proceed in this manner till you have done as many eggs as you wish to preserve; then pack them away in sawdust. We have tried this method of preserving eggs, and can vouch for its excellence. They will be found, at the end of 2 or 3 months, quite good enough for culinary purposes; and although the white may be a little tougher than that of a new-laid egg, the yolk will be nearly the same. Many persons keep eggs for a long time by smearing the shells with butter or sweet oil: they should then be packed in plenty of bran or sawdust, and the eggs not allowed to touch each other. Eggs for storing should be collected in fine weather, and should not be more than 24 hours old when they are packed away, or their flavour, when used, cannot be relied on. Another simple way of preserving eggs is to immerse them in lime-water soon after they have been laid, and then to put the vessel containing the lime-water in a cellar or cool outhouse. *Seasonable.*—The best time for preserving eggs is from April to September.

## EGGS, à la Tripe.

*Ingredients.*—8 eggs, ¾ pint of Béchamel sauce, dessertspoonful of finely-minced parsley. *Mode.*—Boil the eggs hard; put them into cold water, peel them, take out the yolks whole, and shred the whites. Make ¾ pint of Béchamel sauce; add the parsley, and, when the sauce is quite hot, put the yolks of the eggs into the middle of the dish, and the shred whites round them; pour over the sauce, and garnish with leaves of puff-paste or fried croûtons. There is no necessity for putting the eggs into the saucepan with the Béchamel; the sauce, being quite hot, will warm the eggs sufficiently.

*Time.*—10 minutes to boil the eggs. *Average cost,* 1*s*. *Sufficient* for 5 or 6 persons. *Seasonable* at any time.

## ELDER WINE.

*Ingredients.*—To every 3 gallons of water allow 1 peck of elderberries; to every gallon of juice allow 3 lbs. of sugar, ½ oz. of ground ginger, 6 cloves, 1 lb. of good Turkey raisins; ¼ pint of brandy to every gallon of wine. To every 9 gallons of wine, 3 or 4 tablespoonfuls of fresh brewer's yeast. *Mode.*—Pour the water, quite boiling, on the elderberries, which should be picked from the stalks, and let these stand covered for 24 hours; then strain the whole through a sieve or bag, breaking the fruit to express all the juice from it. Measure the liquor, and to every gallon allow the above proportion of sugar. Boil the juice and sugar with the ginger, cloves, and raisins for 1 hour, skimming the liquor the whole time; let it stand until milk-warm, then put it into a clean dry cask, with 3 or 4 tablespoonfuls of good fresh yeast to every 9 gallons of wine. Let it ferment for about a fortnight; then add the brandy, bung up the cask, and let it stand some months before it is bottled, when it will be found excellent. A bunch of hops suspended to a string from the bung, some persons say, will preserve the wine good for several years. Elder wine is usually mulled, and served with sippets of toasted bread and a little grated nutmeg. *Time.*—To stand covered for 24 hours; to be boiled 1 hour. *Average cost,* when made at home, 3*s*. 6*d*. per gallon. *Seasonable.*—Make this in September.

## ENDIVE.

This vegetable, so beautiful in appearance, makes an excellent addition to winter salad, when lettuces and other winter salads are not obtainable. It is usually placed in the centre of the dish, and looks remarkably pretty with slices of beetroot, hard-boiled eggs, and curled celery placed round it, so that the colours contrast nicely. In preparing it, carefully wash and cleanse it free from insects, which are generally found near the heart; remove any decayed or dead leaves, and dry it thoroughly by shaking in a cloth. This vegetable may also be served hot, stewed in cream, brown gravy, or butter; but when dressed thus, the sauce it is stewed in should not be very highly seasoned, as that would destroy and overpower the flavour of the vegetable.

*Average cost*, 1*d*. per head. *Sufficient*.—1 head for a salad for 4 persons. *Seasonable* from November to March.

### ENDIVE, à la Française.

*Ingredients*.—6 heads of endive, 1 pint of broth, 3 oz. of fresh butter; salt, pepper, and grated nutmeg to taste. *Mode*.—Wash and boil the endive as in the preceding recipe; chop it rather fine, and put into a stewpan with the broth; boil over a brisk fire until the sauce is all reduced; then put in the butter, pepper, salt, and grated nutmeg (the latter must be very sparingly used); mix all well together, bring it to the boiling point, and serve very hot. *Time*.—10 minutes to boil, 5 minutes to simmer in the broth. *Average cost*, 1*d*. per head. *Sufficient* for 3 or 4 persons. *Seasonable* from November to March.

### ENDIVE, Stewed.

*Ingredients*.—6 heads of endive, salt and water, 1 pint of broth, thickening of butter and flour, 1 tablespoonful of lemon-juice, a small lump of sugar. *Mode*.—Wash and free the endive thoroughly from insects, remove the green part of the leaves, and put it into boiling water, slightly salted. Let it remain for 10 minutes; then take it out, drain it till there is no water remaining, and chop it very fine. Put it into a stewpan with the broth; add a little salt and a lump of sugar, and boil until the endive is perfectly tender. When done, which may be ascertained by squeezing a piece between the thumb and finger, add a thickening of butter and flour and the lemon-juice; let the sauce boil up, and serve. *Time*.—10 minutes to boil, 5 minutes to simmer in the broth. *Average cost*, 1*d*. per head. *Sufficient* for 3 or 4 persons. *Seasonable* from November to March.

### ESPAGNOLE, or Brown Spanish Sauce.

*Ingredients*.—2 slices of lean ham, 1 lb. of veal, 1½ pint of white stock, 2 or 3 sprigs of parsley, ½ a bay-leaf, 2 or 3 sprigs of savoury herbs, 6 green onions, 3 shalots, 2 cloves, 1 blade of mace, 2 glasses of sherry or Madeira, thickening of butter and flour. *Mode*.—Cut up the ham and veal into small square pieces, and put them into a stewpan. Moisten these with ½ pint of the stock, and simmer till the bottom of the stewpan is covered with a nicely-coloured glaze, when put in a few more spoonfuls to detach it. Add the remainder of the stock, with the spices, herbs, shalots, and onions, and simmer very gently for 1 hour. Strain and skim off every particle of fat, and, when required for use, thicken with butter and flour, or with a little roux. Add the wine, and, if necessary, a seasoning of cayenne; when it will be ready to serve. *Time.*—1½ hour. *Average cost*, 2*s.* per pint.

*Note.*—The wine in this sauce may be omitted, and an onion sliced and fried of a nice brown substituted for it. This sauce or gravy is used for many dishes, and with most people is a general favourite.

## FEBRUARY—BILLS OF FARE.

Dinner for 18 persons.

*First Course.*

|  |  |  |
|---|---|---|
| Fried Eels. | Hare Soup, removed by Turbot and Oyster Sauce.<br><br>Vase of Flowers.<br><br>Oyster Soup, removed by Crimped Cod à la Maître d'Hôtel. | Fried Whitings. |

*Second Course.*

```
                  Braised Capon.
                Boiled Ham, garnished.

Roast Fowls, garnished with                    Boiled Fowls and
      Water-cresses.        Vase of             White Sauce.
                           Flowers.

                    Pâté Chaud.
                 Haunch of Mutton.
```

*Entrées.*

```
                  Lark Pudding.

Lobster Patties.     Vase of       Filets de Perdrix.
                    Flowers.

                Fricasseed Chicken.
```

*Third Course.*

```
                   Ducklings,
                  removed by
                  Iced Pudding.
Meringues.                              Cheesecakes.
                  Coffee Cream.
       Orange Jelly.       Clear Jelly.
                    Vase of
                   Flowers.
                  Blancmange.
         Victoria              Gâteau de
        Sandwiches.             Pommes.
                  Partridges,
                  removed by
                 Cabinet Pudding.
```

Dessert and Ices.

## Dinner for 12 persons.

*First Course.*—Soup à la reine; clear gravy soup; brill and lobster sauce; fried smelts. *Entrées.*—Lobster rissoles; beef palates; pork cutlets à la soubise; grilled mushrooms. *Second Course.*—Braised turkey; haunch of mutton; boiled capon and oysters; tongue, garnished with tufts of broccoli; vegetables and salads. *Third Course.*—Wild ducks; plovers; orange jelly; clear jelly; Charlotte Russe; Nesselrode pudding; gâteau de riz; sea-kale; maids of honour; desert and ices.

## Dinner for 10 persons.

*First Course.*—Palestine soup; John Dory, with Dutch sauce; red mullet, with sauce Génoise. *Entrées.*—Sweetbread cutlets, with poivrade sauce; fowl au Béchamel. *Second Course.*—Roast saddle of mutton; boiled capon and oysters; boiled tongue, garnished with Brussels sprouts. *Third Course.*—Guinea-fowls; ducklings; pain de rhubarb; orange jelly; strawberry cream; cheesecakes; almond pudding; fig pudding; dessert and ices.

## Dinner for 8 persons.

*First Course.*—Mock turtle soup; fillets of turbot à la crême; fried filleted soles and anchovy sauce. *Entrées.*—Larded fillets of rabbits; tendrons de veau with purée of tomatoes. *Second Course.*—Stewed rump of beef à la Jardinière; roast fowls; boiled ham. *Third Course.*—Roast pigeons or larks; rhubarb tartlets; meringues; clear jelly; cream; ice pudding; soufflé; dessert and ices.

## Dinners for 6 persons.

*First Course.*—Rice soup; red mullet, with Génoise sauce; fried smelts. *Entrées.*—Fowl pudding; sweetbreads. *Second Course.*—Roast turkey and sausages; boiled leg of pork; pease pudding. *Third Course.*—Lemon jelly; Charlotte à la vanille; maids of honour; plum-pudding, removed by ice pudding; dessert.

*First Course.*—Spring soup; boiled turbot and lobster sauce. *Entrées.*—Fricasseed rabbit; oyster patties. *Second Course.*—Boiled round of beef and marrow-bones; roast fowls, garnished with water-cresses and rolled bacon; vegetables. *Third Course.*—Marrow pudding; cheesecakes; tartlets of greengage jam; lemon cream; rhubarb tart; dessert.

---

*First Course.*—Vermicelli soup; fried whitings; stewed eels. *Entrées.*—Poulet à la Marengo; breast of veal stuffed and rolled. *Second Course.*—Roast leg of pork and apple sauce; boiled capon and oysters; tongue, garnished with tufts of broccoli. *Third Course.*—Wild ducks; lobster salad; Charlotte aux pommes; pain de rhubarb; vanilla cream; orange jelly; dessert.

*First Course.*—Ox-tail soup; cod à la crême; fried soles. *Entrées.*—Lark pudding; fowl scollops. *Second Course.*—Roast leg of mutton; boiled turkey and celery sauce; pigeon pie; small ham, boiled and garnished; vegetables. *Third Course.*—Game, when liked; tartlets of raspberry jam; vol-au-vent of rhubarb; Swiss cream; cabinet pudding; broccoli and sea-kale; dessert.

## FEBRUARY, Plain Family Dinners for.

*Sunday.*—1. Ox-tail soup. 2. Roast beef, Yorkshire pudding, broccoli, potatoes. 3. Plum-pudding, apple tart. Cheese.

*Monday.*—1. Fried soles, plain melted butter, and potatoes. 2. Cold roast beef, mashed potatoes. 3. The remains of plum-pudding cut in slices, warmed, and served with sifted sugar sprinkled over it. Cheese.

*Tuesday.*—1. The remains of ox-tail soup from Sunday. 2. Pork cutlets with tomato sauce; hashed beef. 3. Rolled jam pudding. Cheese.

*Wednesday.*—1. Boiled haddock and plain melted butter. 2. Rump-steak pudding, potatoes, greens. 3. Arrowroot, blancmange, garnished with jam.

*Thursday.*—1. Boiled leg of pork, greens, potatoes, pease pudding. 2. Apple fritters, sweet macaroni.

*Friday.*—1. Pea-soup made with liquor that the pork was boiled in. 2. Cold pork, mashed potatoes. 3. Baked rice pudding.

*Saturday.*—1. Broiled herrings and mustard sauce. 2. Haricot mutton. 3. Macaroni, either served as a sweet pudding or with cheese.

---

*Sunday.*—1. Carrot soup. 2. Boiled leg of mutton and caper sauce, mashed turnips, roast fowls, and bacon. 3. Damson tart made with bottled fruit, ratafia pudding.

*Monday.*—1. The remainder of fowl curried and served with rice; rump-steaks and oyster sauce, cold mutton. 2. Rolled jam pudding.

*Tuesday.*—1. Vegetable soup made with liquor the mutton was boiled in on Sunday. 2. Roast sirloin of beef, Yorkshire pudding, broccoli, and potatoes. 3. Cheese.

*Wednesday.*—1. Fried soles, melted butter. Cold beef and mashed potatoes; if there is any cold mutton left, cut it into neat slices and warm it in a little caper sauce. 2. Apple tart.

*Thursday.*—1. Boiled rabbit and onion sauce, stewed beef and vegetables, made with the remains of cold beef and bones. 2. Macaroni.

*Friday.*—1. Roast leg of pork, sage and onions and apple sauce, greens and potatoes. 2. Spinach and poached eggs instead of pudding. Cheese and water-cresses.

*Saturday.*—1. Rump-steak and kidney pudding, cold pork and mashed potatoes. 2. Baked rice pudding.

## FEBRUARY, Things in Season.

*Fish.*—Barbel, brill, carp; cod may be bought, but is not so good as in January; crabs, crayfish, dace, eels, flounders, haddocks, herrings, lampreys, lobsters, mussels, oysters, perch, pike, place, prawns, shrimps, skate, smelts, soles, sprats, sturgeon, tench, thornback, turbot, whiting.

*Meat.*—Beef, house lamb, mutton, pork, veal.

*Poultry.*—Capons, chickens, ducklings, tame and wild pigeons, pullets with eggs, turkeys, wild-fowl, though now not in full season.

*Game.*—Grouse, hares, partridges, pheasants, snipes, woodcock.

*Vegetables.*—Beetroot, broccoli (purple and white), Brussels sprouts, cabbages, carrots, celery, chervil, cresses, cucumbers (forced), endive, kidney-beans, lettuces, parsnips, potatoes, savoys, spinach, turnips—various herbs.

*Fruit.*—Apples (golden and Dutch pippins), grapes, medlars, nuts, oranges, pears (Bon Chrétien), walnuts, dried fruits (foreign), such as almonds and raisins; French and Spanish plums; prunes, figs, dates, crystallized preserves.

## FENNEL SAUCE, for Mackerel.

*Ingredients.*—½ pint of melted butter, rather more than 1 tablespoonful of chopped fennel. *Mode.*—Make the melted butter very smooth, chop the fennel rather small, carefully cleansing it from any grit or dirt, and put it to the butter when this is on the point of boiling. Simmer for a minute or two, and serve in a tureen. *Time.*—2 minutes. *Average cost*, 4d. *Sufficient* to serve with 5 or 6 mackerel.

## FIG PUDDING.

*Ingredients.*—2 lbs. of figs, 1 lb. of suet, ½ lb. of flour, ½ lb. of bread-crumbs, 2 eggs, milk. *Mode.*—Cut the figs into small pieces, grate the bread finely, and chop the suet very small; mix these well together, add the flour, the eggs, which should be well beaten, and sufficient milk to form the whole into a stiff paste; butter a mould or basin, press the pudding into it very closely, tie it down with a cloth, and boil for 3 hours, or rather longer; turn it out of the mould, and serve with melted butter, wine-sauce, or cream. *Time.*—3 hours, or longer. *Average cost*, 2s. *Sufficient* for 7 or 8 persons. *Seasonable.*—Suitable for a winter pudding.

## FIG PUDDING (Staffordshire Recipe).

*Ingredients.*—1 lb. of figs, 6 oz. of suet, ¾ lb. of flour, milk. *Mode.*—Chop the suet finely, mix with it the flour, and make these into a smooth paste with milk; roll it out to the thickness of about ½ inch, cut the figs in small pieces, and strew them over the paste; roll it up, make the ends secure, tie the pudding in a cloth, and boil it from 1½ to 2 hours. *Time.*—1½ to 2 hours. *Average cost*, 1s. 1d. *Sufficient* for 5 or 6 persons. *Seasonable* at any time.

## FIGS, Compôte of Green.

*Ingredients.*—1 pint of syrup, 1½ pint of green figs, the rind of ½ lemon. *Mode.*—Make a syrup as directed, boiling with it the lemon-rind, and carefully remove all the scum as it rises. Put in the figs, and simmer them very slowly until tender; dish them on a glass dish; reduce the syrup by boiling it quickly for 5 minutes; take out the lemon-peel, pour the syrup over the figs, and the compôte, when cold, will be ready for table. A little port wine, or lemon-juice, added just before the figs are done, will be found an improvement. *Time.*—2 to 3 hours to stew the figs. *Average cost*, figs, 2s. to 3s. per dozen. *Seasonable* in August and September.

**COMPÔTE OF FIGS.**

## FISH.

Fish shortly before they spawn are, in general, best in condition. When the spawning is just over, they are out of season, and unfit for human food.

When fish is out of season, it has a transparent, bluish tinge, however much it may be boiled; whenever it is in season, its muscles are firm, and boil white and curdy.

As food for invalids, white fish, such as the ling, cod, haddock, coal-fish, and whiting, are the best; flat fish, as soles, skate, turbot, and flounders, are also good.

Salmon, mackerel, herrings, and trout soon spoil or decompose after they are killed; therefore, to be in perfection, they should be prepared for the table on the day they are caught. With flat fish, this is not of such consequence, as they will keep longer. The turbot, for example, is improved by being kept for a few hours.

## FISH, General Directions for Dressing.

In dressing fish of any kind, the first point to be attended to, is to see that it is perfectly clean. It is a common error to wash it too much, as by doing so the flavour is diminished. If the fish is to be boiled, a little salt and vinegar should be put into the water, to give it firmness, after it is cleaned. Codfish, whiting, and haddock, are none the worse for being a little salted, and kept a day; and, if the weather be not very hot, they will be good for two days.

When fish is cheap and plentiful, and a larger quantity is purchased than is immediately wanted, the overplus of such as will bear it should be potted, or pickled, or salted, and hung up; or it may be fried, that it may serve for stewing the next day. Fresh-water fish, having frequently a muddy smell and taste, should be soaked in strong salt and water, after it has been well cleaned. If of a sufficient size, it may be scalded in salt and water, and afterwards dried and dressed.

Fish should be put into cold water and set on the fire to do very gently, or the outside will break before the inner part is done. Unless the fishes are small, they should never be put into warm water; nor should water, either hot or cold, be poured *on* to the fish, as it is liable to break the skin; if it should be necessary to add a little water whilst the fish is cooking, it ought to be poured in gently at the side of the vessel. The fish-plate may be drawn up, to see if the fish be ready, which may be known by its easily separating from the bone. It should then be immediately taken out of the water, or it will become woolly. The fish-plate should be set crossways over the kettle, to keep hot for serving, and a cloth laid over the fish, to prevent its losing its colour.

In garnishing fish great attention is required, and plenty of parsley, horseradish, and lemon should be used. If fried parsley be used, it must be washed and picked, and thrown into fresh water. When the lard or dripping boils, throw the parsley into it immediately from the water, and instantly it will be green and crisp, and must be taken up with a slice. When well done, and with very good sauce, fish is more appreciated than almost any other dish. The liver and roe, in some instances, should be placed on the dish, in order that they may be distributed in the course of serving; but to each recipe will be appended the proper mode of serving and garnishing.

If fish is to be fried or broiled it must be dried in a nice soft cloth after it is well cleaned and washed. If for frying, brush it over with egg, and sprinkle it with some fine crumbs of bread. If done a second time with the egg and bread, the fish will look so much the better. If required to be very nice, a sheet of white blotting-paper must be placed to receive it, that it may be free from all grease; it must also be of a beautiful colour, and all the crumbs appear distinct. Butter gives a bad colour; lard and clarified dripping are most frequently used; but oil is the best, if the expense be no objection. The fish should be put into the lard when boiling, and there should be a sufficiency of this to cover it.

When fish is broiled, it must be seasoned, floured, and laid on a very clean gridiron, which, when hot, should be rubbed with a bit of suet, to prevent the fish from sticking. It must be broiled over a very clear fire, that it may not taste smoky; and not too near, that it may not be scorched.

In choosing fish, it is well to remember that it is possible it may be *fresh*, and yet not *good*. Under the head of each particular fish in this work, are appended rules for its choice, and the months when it is in season. Nothing can be of greater consequence to a cook than to have the fish good; as, if this important course in a dinner does not give satisfaction, it is rarely that the repast goes off well.

## FISH, General Directions for Carving.

In carving fish, care should be taken to help it in perfect flakes, as, if these are broken, the beauty of the fish is lost. The carver should be acquainted, too, with the choicest parts and morsels; and to give each guest an equal share of these *titbits* should be his maxim. Steel knives and forks should on no account be used in helping fish, as these are liable to impart to it a very disagreeable flavour. When silver fish-carvers are considered too dear to be bought, good electro-plated ones answer very well, and are inexpensive.

## FISH CAKE.

*Ingredients.*—The remains of any cold fish, 1 onion, 1 faggot of sweet herbs; salt and pepper to taste, 1 pint of water, equal quantities of bread-crumbs and cold potatoes, ½ teaspoonful of parsley, 1 egg, bread-crumbs. *Mode.*—Pick the meat from the bones of the fish, which latter put, with the head and fins, into a stewpan with the water; add pepper and salt, the onion and herbs, and stew slowly for gravy about 2 hours; chop the fish fine, and mix it well with bread-crumbs and cold potatoes, adding the parsley and seasoning; make the whole into a cake with the white of an egg, brush it over with egg, cover with bread-crumbs, fry of a light brown; strain the gravy, pour it over, and stew gently for ¼ of an hour, stirring it carefully once or twice. Serve hot, and garnish with thin slices of lemon and parsley. *Time.*—½ an hour after the gravy is made.

## FISH AND OYSTER PIE.

[COLD MEAT COOKERY.] *Ingredients.*—Any remains of cold fish, such as cod or haddock; 2 dozen oysters, pepper and salt to taste, bread-crumbs sufficient for the quantity of fish; ½ teaspoonful of grated nutmeg, 1 teaspoonful of finely-chopped parsley. *Mode.*—Clear the fish from the bones, and put a layer of it in a pie-dish, which sprinkle with pepper and salt; then a layer of bread-crumbs, oysters, nutmeg, and chopped parsley. Repeat this till the dish is quite full. You may form a covering either of bread-crumbs, which should be browned, or puff-paste, which should be cut into long strips, and laid in cross-bars over the fish, with a line of the paste first laid round the edge. Before putting on the top, pour in some made melted butter, or a little thin white sauce, and the oyster-liquor, and bake. *Time.*—If made of cooked fish, ¼ hour; if made of fresh fish and puff-paste, ¾ hour. *Average cost*, 1*s*. 6*d*. *Seasonable* from September to April.

*Note.*—A nice little dish may be made by flaking any cold fish, adding a few oysters, seasoning with pepper and salt, and covering with mashed potatoes; ¼ hour will bake it.

## FISH PIE, with Tench and Eels.

*Ingredients.*—2 tench, 2 eels, 2 onions, a faggot of herbs, 4 blades of mace, 3 anchovies, 1 pint of water, pepper and salt to taste, 1 teaspoonful of chopped parsley, the yokes of 6 hard-boiled eggs, puff-paste. *Mode.*—Clean and bone the tench, skin and bone the eels, and cut them into pieces 2 inches long, and leave the sides of the tench whole. Put the bones into a stewpan with the onions, herbs, mace, anchovies, water, and seasoning, and let them simmer gently for 1 hour. Strain it off, put it to cool, and skim off all the fat. Lay the tench and eels in a pie-dish, and between each layer put seasoning, chopped parsley, and hard-boiled eggs; pour in part of the strained liquor, cover in with puff-paste, and bake for ½ hour or rather more. The oven should be rather quick, and when done, heat the remainder of the liquor, which pour into the pie. *Time.*—½ hour to bake, or rather more if the oven is slow.

## FISH SAUCE.

*Ingredients.*—1½ oz. of cayenne, 2 tablespoonfuls of walnut ketchup, 2 tablespoonfuls of soy, a few shreds of garlic and shalot, 1 quart of vinegar. *Mode.*—Put all the ingredients into a large bottle, and shake well every day for a fortnight. Keep it in small bottles well sealed, and in a few days it will be fit for use. *Average cost*, for this quantity, 1*s*.

## FISH, Scalloped.

[COLD MEAT COOKERY.] *Ingredients.*—Remains of cold fish of any sort, ½ pint of cream, ½ tablespoonful of anchovy sauce, ½ teaspoonful of made mustard, ditto of walnut ketchup, pepper and salt to taste (the above quantities are for ½ lb. of fish when picked): bread-crumbs. *Mode.*—Put all the ingredients into a stewpan, carefully picking the fish from the bones; set it on the fire, let it remain till nearly hot, occasionally stir the contents, but do not allow it to boil. When done, put the fish into a deep dish or scallop shell, with a good quantity of bread-crumbs; place small pieces of butter on the top, set in a Dutch oven before the fire to brown, or use a salamander. *Time.*—¼ hour. *Average cost*, exclusive of the cold fish, 10*d*.

## FISH, Scalloped.

[COLD MEAT COOKERY.] *Ingredients.*—Any cold fish, 1 egg, milk, 1 large blade of pounded mace, 1 tablespoonful of flour, 1 teaspoonful of anchovy sauce, pepper and salt to taste, bread-crumbs, butter. *Mode.*—Pick the fish carefully from the bones, and moisten with milk and the egg; add the other ingredients, and place in a deep ditch or scallop shells; over with bread-crumbs, butter the top, and brown before the fire; when quite hot, serve. *Time.*—20 minutes. *Average cost*, exclusive of the cold fish, 4*d*.

## FISH STOCK.

*Ingredients.*—2 lbs. of beef or veal (these can be omitted), any kind of white fish trimmings of fish which are to be dressed for table, 2 onions, the rind of ½ a lemon, a bunch of sweet herbs, 2 carrots, 2 quarts of water. *Mode.*—Cut up the fish, and put it, with the other ingredients, into the water. Simmer for 2 hours; skim the liquor carefully, and strain it. When a richer stock is wanted, fry the vegetables and fish before adding the water. *Time.*—2 hours. *Average cost*, with meat, 10*d*. per quart; without, 3*d*.

*Note.*—Do not make fish stock long before it is wanted, as it soon turns sour.

## FLOUNDERS, Boiled.

*Ingredients.*—Sufficient water to cover the flounders, salt in the proportion of 6 oz. to each gallon, a little vinegar. *Mode.*—Put on a kettle with enough water to cover the flounders, lay in the fish, add salt and vinegar in the above proportions, and when it boils, simmer very gently for 5 minutes. They must not boil fast, or they will break. Serve with plain melted butter, or parsley and butter. *Time.*—After the water boils, 5 minutes. *Average cost*, 3*d*. each. *Seasonable* from August to November.

## FLOUNDERS, Fried.

*Ingredients.*—Flounders, egg, and bread-crumbs; boiling lard. *Mode.*—Cleanse the fish, and, two hours before they are wanted, rub them inside and out with salt, to render them firm; wash and wipe them very dry, dip them into egg, and sprinkle over with bread-crumbs; fry them in boiling lard, dish on a hot napkin, and garnish with crisped parsley. *Time.*—From 5 to 10 minutes, according to size. *Average cost,* 3*d.* each. *Seasonable* from August to November. *Sufficient,* 1 for each person.

## FLOWERS, Almond.

*Ingredients.*—Puff-paste; to every ½ lb. of paste allow 3 oz. of almonds, sifted sugar, the white of an egg. *Mode.*—Roll the paste out to the thickness of ¼ inch, and, with a round fluted cutter, stamp out as many pieces as may be required. Work the paste up again, roll it out, and, with a smaller cutter, stamp out some pieces the size of a shilling. Brush the larger pieces over with the white of an egg, and place one of the smaller pieces on each. Blanch and cut the almonds into strips lengthwise; press them slanting into the paste closely round the rings; and when they are all completed, sift over some pounded sugar, and bake for about ¼ hour or twenty minutes. Garnish between the almonds with strips of apple jelly, and place in centre of the ring a small quantity of strawberry jam; pile them high on the dish, and serve. *Time.*—¼ hour or 20 minutes. *Sufficient.*—18 or 20 for a dish. *Seasonable* at any time.

## FLOWERS, to Preserve Cut.

A bouquet of freshly-cut flowers may be preserved alive for a long time by placing them in a glass or vase with fresh water, in which a little charcoal has been steeped, or a small piece of camphor dissolved. The vase should be set upon a plate or dish, and covered with a bell-glass, around the edges of which, when it comes in contact with the plate, a little water should be poured to exclude the air.

## FLOWERS, to Revive after Packing.

Plunge the stems into boiling water, and, by the time the water is cold, the flowers will have revived. Then cut afresh the ends of the stems, and keep them in fresh cold water.

## FONDUE.

*Ingredients.*—4 eggs, the weight of 2 in Parmesan or good Cheshire cheese, the weight of 2 in butter; pepper and salt to taste. *Mode.*—Separate the yolks from the whites of the eggs; beat the former in a basin, and grate the cheese, or cut it into *very thin* flakes. Parmesan or Cheshire cheese may be used, whichever is the most convenient, although the former is considered more suitable for this dish; or an equal quantity of each may be used. Break the butter into small pieces, add to it the other ingredients, with sufficient pepper and salt to season nicely, and beat the mixture thoroughly. Well whisk the whites of the eggs, stir them lightly in, and either bake the fondue in a soufflé-dish or small round cake-tin. Fill the dish only half full, as the fondue should rise very much. Pin a napkin round the tin or dish, and serve very hot and very quickly. If allowed to stand after it is withdrawn from the oven, the beauty and lightness of this preparation will be entirely spoiled. *Time.*—From 15 to 20 minutes. *Average cost*, 10*d*. *Sufficient* for 4 or 5 persons. *Seasonable* at any time.

## FONDUE, Brillat Savarin's (an excellent Recipe).

*Ingredients.*—Eggs, cheese, butter, pepper and salt. *Mode.*—Take the same number of eggs as there are guests; weigh the eggs in the shell, allow a third of their weight in Gruyère cheese, and a piece of butter one-sixth of the weight of the cheese. Break the eggs into a basin, beat them well; add the cheese, which should be grated, and the butter, which should be broken into small pieces. Stir these ingredients together with a wooden spoon; put the mixture into a lined saucepan, place it over the fire, and stir until the substance is thick and soft. Put in a little salt, according to the age of the cheese, and a good sprinkling of pepper, and serve the fondue on a very hot silver or metal plate. Do not allow the fondue to remain on the fire after the mixture is set, as, if it boils, it will be entirely spoiled. Brillat Savarin recommends that some choice Burgundy should be handed round with this dish. We have given this recipe exactly as he recommends it to be made; but we have tried it with good Cheshire cheese, and found it answer remarkably well. *Time.*—About 4 minutes to set the mixture. *Average cost*, for 4 persons, 10*d*. *Sufficient.*—Allow 1 egg, with the other ingredients in proportion, for 1 person. *Seasonable* at any time.

## FOOD FOR INFANTS, and its Preparation.

The articles generally employed as food for infants consist of arrowroot, bread, flour, baked flour, prepared groats, farinaceous food, biscuit-powder, biscuits, tops-and-bottoms, and semolina, or manna croup, as it is otherwise called, which, like tapioca, is the prepared pith of certain vegetable substances. Of this list the least efficacious, though, perhaps, the most believed in, is arrowroot, which only as a mere agent, for change, and then only for a very short time, should ever be employed as a means of diet to infancy or childhood. It is a thin, flatulent, and innutritious food, and incapable of supporting infantine life and energy. Bread, though the universal *régime* with the labouring poor, where the infant's stomach and digestive powers are a reflex, in miniature, of the father's, should never be given to an infant under three months, and, even then, however finely beaten up and smoothly made, is a very questionable diet. Flour, when well boiled, though infinitely better than arrowroot, is still only a kind of fermentative paste, that counteracts its own good by after-acidity and flatulence.

Baked flour, when cooked into a pale brown mass, and finely powdered, makes a far superior food to the others, and may be considered as a very useful diet, especially for a change. Prepared groats may be classed with arrowroot and raw flour, as being innutritious. The articles that now follow on our list are all good, and such as we could, with conscience and safety, trust to the health and development of any child whatever.

We may observe in this place, that an occasional change in the character of the food is highly desirable, both as regards the health and benefit of the child; and, though the interruption should only last for a day, the change will be advantageous.

The packets sold as farinaceous food are unquestionably the best aliment that can be given from the first to a baby, and may be continued, with the exception of an occasional change, without alteration of the material, till the child is able to take its regular meals of animal and vegetable food. Some infants are so constituted as to require a frequent and a total change in their system of living, seeming to thrive for a certain time on any food given to them, but if persevered in too long, declining in bulk and appearance as rapidly as they had previously progressed. In such cases, the food should be immediately changed, and when that which appeared to agree best with the child is resumed, it should be altered in its quality, and perhaps in its consistency.

For the farinaceous food there are directions with each packet, containing instructions for the making; but, whatever the food employed is, enough should be made at once to last the day and night; at first, about a pint basinful, but, as the child advances, a quart will hardly be too much. In all cases, let the food boil a sufficient time, constantly stirring, and taking every precaution that it does not get burnt, in which case it is on no account to be used.

The food should always be made with water, the whole sweetened at once, and of such a consistency that, when poured out, and it has had time to cool, it will cut with the firmness of a pudding or custard. One or two spoonfuls are to be put into the pap saucepan and stood on the hob till the heat has softened it, when enough milk is to be added, and carefully mixed with the food, till the whole has the consistency of ordinary cream; it is then to be poured into the nursing-bottle, and the food having been drawn through to warm the nipple, it is to be placed in the child's mouth. For the first month or more, half a bottleful will be quite enough to give the infant at one time; but, as the child grows, it will be necessary not only to increase the quantity given at each time, but also gradually to make its food more consistent, and, after the third month, to add an egg to every pint basin of food made. At night, the mother puts the food into the covered pan of her lamp, instead of the saucepan—that is, enough for one supply, and, having lighted the rush, she will find, on the waking of her child, the food sufficiently hot to bear the cooling addition of the milk. But, whether night or day, the same food should never be heated twice, and what the child leaves should be thrown away.

The biscuit powder is used in the same manner as the farinaceous food, and both prepared much after the fashion of making starch. But when tops-and-bottoms, or the whole biscuit, are employed, they require soaking in cold water for some time previously to boiling. The biscuit or biscuits are then to be slowly boiled in as much water as will, when thoroughly soft, allow of their being beaten by a three-pronged fork into a fine, smooth, and even pulp, and which, when poured into a basin and become cold, will cut out like a custard. If two large biscuits have been so treated, and the child is six or seven months old, beat up two eggs, sufficient sugar to properly sweeten it, and about a pint of skim milk. Pour this on the beaten biscuit in the saucepan, stirring constantly; boil for about five minutes, pour into a basin, and use, when cold, in the same manner as the other.

This makes an admirable food, at once nutritious and strengthening. When tops-and-bottoms or rusks are used, the quantity of the egg may be reduced, or altogether omitted.

Semolina, or manna croup, being in little hard grains, like a fine millet-seed, must be boiled for some time, and the milk, sugar, and egg added to it on the fire, and boiled for a few minutes longer, and, when cold, used as the other preparations.

Many persons entertain a belief that cow's milk is hurtful to infants, and, consequently, refrain from giving it; but this is a very great mistake, for both sugar and milk should form a large portion of every meal an infant takes.

## FORCEMEATS.

The points which cooks should, in this branch of cookery, more particularly observe, are the thorough chopping of the suet, the complete mincing of the herbs, the careful grating of the bread-crumbs, and the perfect mixing of the whole. These are the three principal ingredients of forcemeats, and they can scarcely be cut too small, as nothing like a lump or fibre should be anywhere perceptible. To conclude, the flavour of no one spice or herb should be permitted to predominate.

## FORCEMEAT BALLS, for Fish Soups.

*Ingredients.*—1 middling-sized lobster, ½ an anchovy, 1 head of boiled celery, the yolk of a hard-boiled egg; salt, cayenne, and mace to taste; 4 tablespoonfuls of bread-crumbs, 2 oz. of butter, 2 eggs. *Mode.*—Pick the meat from the shell of the lobster, and pound it, with the soft parts, in a mortar; add the celery, the yolk of the hard-boiled egg, seasoning, and bread-crumbs. Continue pounding till the whole is nicely amalgamated. Warm the butter till it is in a liquid state; well whisk the eggs, and work these up with the pounded lobster-meat. Make the balls of about an inch in diameter, and fry of a nice pale brown. *Sufficient*, from 18 to 20 balls for 1 tureen of soup.

## FORCEMEAT, French.

It will be well to state, in the beginning of this recipe, that French forcemeat, or quenelles, consist of the blending of three separate processes; namely, panada, udder, and whatever meat you intend using.

**Panada.** *Ingredients.*—The crumb of 2 penny rolls, 4 tablespoonfuls of white stock, 1 oz. of butter, 1 slice of ham, 1 bay-leaf, a little minced parsley, 2 shalots, 1 clove, 2 blades of mace, a few mushrooms, butter, the yolks of 2 eggs. *Mode.*—Soak the crumb of the rolls in milk for about ½ hour, then take it out, and squeeze so as to press the milk from it; put the soaked bread into a stewpan with the above quantity of white stock, and set it on one side; then put into a separate stewpan 1 oz. of butter, a slice of lean ham cut small, with a bay-leaf, herbs, mushrooms, spices, &c., in the above proportions, and fry them gently over a slow fire. When done, moisten with 2 teacupfuls of white stock, boil for 20 minutes, and strain the whole through a sieve over the panada in the other stewpan. Place it over the fire, keep constantly stirring, to prevent its burning, and, when quite dry, put in a small piece of butter. Let this again dry up by stirring over the fire; then add the yolks of 2 eggs, mix well, put the panada to cool on a clean plate, and use it when required. Panada should always be well flavoured, as the forcemeat receives no taste from any of the other ingredients used in its preparation.

**Boiled Calf's Udder for French Forcemeat.**—Put the udder into a stewpan with sufficient water to cover it; let it stew gently till quite done, when take it out to cool. Trim all the upper parts, cut it into small pieces, and pound well in a mortar, till it can be rubbed through a sieve. That portion which passes through the strainer is one of the three ingredients of which French forcemeats are generally composed; but many cooks substitute butter for this, being a less troublesome and more expeditious mode of preparation.

## FORCEMEAT, for Cold Savoury Pies.

*Ingredients.*—1 lb. of veal, 1 lb. of fat bacon; salt, cayenne, pepper, and pounded mace to taste; a very little nutmeg, the same of chopped lemon-peel, ½ teaspoonful of chopped parsley, ½ teaspoonful of minced savoury herbs, 1 or 2 eggs. *Mode.*—Chop the veal and bacon together, and put them into a mortar with the other ingredients mentioned above. Pound well, and bind with 1 or 2 eggs which have been previously beaten and strained. Work the whole well together, and the forcemeat will be ready for use. If the pie is not to be eaten immediately, omit the herbs and parsley, as these will prevent it from keeping. Mushrooms or truffles may be added. *Sufficient* for 2 small pies.

## FORCEMEAT, for Pike, Carp, Haddock, and various Kinds of Fish.

*Ingredients.*—1 oz. of fresh butter, 1 oz. of suet, 1 oz. of fat bacon, 1 small teaspoonful of minced savoury herbs, including parsley; a little onion, when liked, shredded very fine; salt, nutmeg, and cayenne to taste; 4 oz. of bread-crumbs, 1 egg. *Mode.*—Mix all the ingredients well together, carefully mincing them very finely; beat up the egg, moisten with it, and work the whole very smoothly together. Oysters or anchovies may be added to this forcemeat, and will be found a great improvement. *Average cost*, 6d. *Sufficient* for a moderate-sized haddock or pie.

## FORCEMEAT, for Baked Pike.

*Ingredients.*—3 oz. of bread-crumbs, 1 teaspoonful of minced savoury herbs, 8 oysters, 2 anchovies (these may be dispensed with), 2 oz. of suet; salt, pepper, and pounded mace to taste; 6 tablespoonfuls of cream or milk, the yolks of 2 eggs. *Mode.*—Beard and mince the oysters, prepare and mix the other ingredients, and blend the whole thoroughly together. Moisten with the cream and eggs, put all into a stewpan, and stir it over the fire till it thickens, when put it into the fish, which should have previously been cut open, and sew it up. *Time.*—4 or 5 minutes to thicken. *Average cost*, 10d. *Sufficient* for a moderate-sized pike.

## FORCEMEAT, or QUENELLES, for Turtle Soup. (Soyer's Recipe.)

Take a pound and a half of lean veal from the fillet, and cut it in long thin slices; scrape with a knife till nothing but the fibre remains; put it into a mortar, pound it 10 minutes, or until in a purée; pass it through a wire sieve (use the remainder in stock); then take 1 pound of good fresh beef suet, which skin, shred, and chop very fine; put it into a mortar and pound it; then add 6 oz. of panada (that is, bread soaked in milk and boiled till nearly dry) with the suet; pound them well together, and add the veal; season with a teaspoonful of salt, a quarter one of pepper, half that of nutmeg; work all well together; then add four eggs by degrees, continually pounding the contents of the mortar. When well mixed, take a small piece in a spoon, and poach it in some boiling water; and if it is delicate, firm, and of a good flavour, it is ready for use.

## FORCEMEAT VEAL, or VEAL QUENELLES.

*Ingredients.*—Equal quantities of veal, panada, and calf's udder, 2 eggs; seasoning to taste of pepper, salt, and pounded mace, or grated nutmeg; a little flour. *Mode.*—Take the fleshy part of veal, scrape it with a knife, till all the meat is separated from the sinews, and allow about ½ lb. for an entrée. Chop the meat, and pound it in a mortar till reduced to a paste; then roll it into a ball; make another of panada the same size, and another of udder, taking care that these three balls be of the same size. (It is to be remembered, that equality of *size*, and not of weight, is here necessary.) When the three ingredients are properly prepared, pound them altogether in a mortar for some time; for the more quenelles are pounded, the more delicate they are. Now moisten with the eggs, whites and yolks, and continue pounding, adding a seasoning of pepper, spices, &c. When the whole is well blended together, mould it into balls, or whatever shape is intended, roll them in flour, and poach in boiling water, to which a little salt should have been added. If the quenelles are not firm enough, add the yolk of another egg, but omit the white, which only makes them hollow and puffy inside. In the preparation of this recipe, it would be well to bear in mind that the ingredients are to be well pounded and seasoned, and must be made hard or soft according to the dishes they are intended for. For brown or white ragoûts they should be firm, and when the quenelles are used very small, extreme delicacy will be necessary in their preparation. Their flavour may be varied by using the flesh of rabbit, fowl, hare, pheasant, grouse, or an extra quantity of mushroom, parsley, &c.

## FORCEMEAT for Veal, Turkeys, Fowls, Hare, &c.

*Ingredients.*—2 oz. of ham or lean bacon, ¼ lb. of suet, the rind of half a lemon, 1 teaspoonful of minced parsley, 1 teaspoonful of minced sweet herbs; salt, cayenne, and pounded mace to taste; 6 oz. of bread-crumbs, 2 eggs. *Mode.*—Shred the ham or bacon, chop the suet, lemon-peel, and herbs, taking particular care that all be very finely minced; add a seasoning to taste of salt, cayenne, and mace, and blend all thoroughly together with the bread-crumbs, before wetting. Now beat and strain the eggs; work these up with the other ingredients, and the forcemeat will be ready for use. When it is made into balls, fry of a nice brown, in boiling lard, or put them on a tin and bake for ½ hour in a moderate oven. As we have stated before, no one flavour should predominate greatly, and the forcemeat should be of sufficient body to cut with a knife, and yet not dry and heavy. For very delicate forcemeat, it is advisable to pound the ingredients together before binding with the eggs; but for ordinary cooking, mincing very finely answers the purpose. *Average cost*, 8d. *Sufficient* for a turkey, a moderate-sized fillet of veal, or a hare.

*Note.*—In the forcemeat for Hare, the liver of the animal is sometimes added. Boil for 5 minutes, mince it very small, and mix it with the other ingredients. If it should be in an unsound state, it must be on no account made use of.

## FOWLS, Boiled, à la Béchamel.

*Ingredients.*—A pair of fowls, 1 pint of Béchamel, a few bunches of boiled broccoli or cauliflower. *Mode.*—Truss and boil the flowers; make a pint of Béchamel sauce; pour some of this over the fowls, and the remainder send to table in a tureen. Garnish the dish with bunches of boiled cauliflowers or broccoli, and serve very hot. The sauce should be made sufficiently thick to adhere to the fowls; that for the tureen should be thinned by adding a spoonful or two of stock. *Time.*—From ½ to 1 hour, according to size. *Average cost*, in full season, 5s. a pair. *Sufficient* for 6 or 7 persons. *Seasonable* all the year, but scarce in early spring.

**BOILED FOWL.**

**LEG, WING, AND NECKBONE OF FOWL.**

This will not be found a very difficult member of the poultry family to carve, unless, as may happen, a very old farm-yard occupant, useless for egg-laying purposes, has, by some unlucky mischance, been introduced into the kitchen as a "fine young chicken." Skill, however, and the application of a small amount of strength, combined with a fine keeping of the temper, will even get over that difficulty. Fixing the fork firmly in the breast, let the knife be firmly passed along the line shown from 1 to 2; then cut downwards from that line to fig. 3: and the wing, it will be found, can be easily withdrawn. The shape of the wing should be like the accompanying engraving. Let the fork be placed inside the leg, which should be gently forced away from the body of the fowl; and the joint, being thus discovered, the carver can readily cut through it, and the leg can be served. When the leg is displaced, it should be of the same shape as that shown in the annexed woodcut. The legs and wings on either side having been taken off, the carver should draw his knife through the flesh in the direction of the line 4 to 5; by this means the knife can be slipped underneath the merrythought, which, being lifted up and pressed backward, will immediately come off. The collar- or neck-bones are the next to consider: these lie on each side of the merrythought, close under the upper part of the wings; and, in order to free these from the fowl, they must also be raised by the knife at their broad end, and turned from the body towards the breastbone, until the shorter piece of the bone, as shown in the cut, breaks off. There will now be left only the breast, with the ribs. The breast can be, without difficulty, disengaged from the ribs by cutting through the latter, which will offer little impediment. The side bones are now to be taken off; and to do this, the lower end of the back should be turned from the carver, who should press the point of the knife through the top of the backbone, near the centre, bringing it down towards the end of the back completely through the bone. If the knife be now turned in the opposite direction, the joint will be easily separated from the vertebræ. The backbone being now uppermost, the fork should be pressed firmly down on it, whilst at the same time the knife should be employed in raising up the lower small end of the fowl towards the fork, and thus the back will be dislocated about its middle. The wings, breast, and merrythought are esteemed the prime parts of a fowl, and are usually served to the ladies of the company, to whom legs, except as a matter of paramount necessity, should not be given. Byron gave it as one reason why he did not like dining with ladies, that they always had the wings of the fowls, which he himself preferred. We heard a gentleman who, when he might have had a wing, declare his partiality for a leg, saying that he had been obliged to eat legs for so long a time that he had at last come to like them better than the other more prized parts. If the fowl is, capon-like, very large, slices may be carved from its breast in the same manner as from a turkey's.

### FOWL, Boiled, with Oysters. (Excellent.)

*Ingredients.*—1 young fowl, 3 dozen oysters, the yolks of 2 eggs, ¼ pint of cream. *Mode.*—Truss a young fowl as for boiling; fill the inside with oysters which have been bearded and washed in their own liquor; secure the ends of the fowl, put it into a jar, and plunge the jar into a saucepan of boiling water. Keep it boiling for 1½ hour, or rather longer; then take the gravy that has flowed from the oysters and fowl, of which there will be a good quantity; stir in the cream and yolks of eggs, add a few oysters scalded in their liquor; let the sauce get quite *hot*, but do not allow it to *boil*; pour some of it over the fowl, and the remainder send to table in a tureen. A blade of pounded mace added to the sauce, with the cream and eggs, will be found an improvement. *Time.*—1½ hour. *Average cost*, 4*s*. 6*d*. *Sufficient* for 3 or 4 persons. *Seasonable* from September to April.

## FOWLS, Broiled, and Mushroom Sauce.

*Ingredients.*—A large fowl; seasoning, to taste, of pepper and salt, 2 handfuls of button mushrooms, 1 slice of lean ham, ¾ pint of thickened gravy, 1 teaspoonful of lemon juice, ½ teaspoonful of pounded sugar. *Mode.*—Cut the fowl into quarters, roast it until three-parts done, and keep it well basted whilst at the fire. Take the fowl up, broil it for a few minutes over a clear fire, and season it with pepper and salt. Have ready some mushroom sauce made in the following manner. Put the mushrooms into a stewpan with a small piece of butter, the ham, a seasoning of pepper and salt, and the gravy; simmer these gently for ½ hour, add the lemon-juice and sugar, dish the fowl, and pour the sauce round them. *Time.*—To roast the fowl, 35 minutes; to broil it, 10 to 15 minutes. *Average cost*, in full season, 2*s*. 6*d*. *Sufficient* for 4 or 5 persons. *Seasonable.*—In full season from May to January.

## FOWL, Boiled, and Rice.

*Ingredients.*—1 fowl, mutton broth, 2 onions, 2 small blades of pounded mace, pepper and salt to taste, ¼ pint of rice, parsley and butter. *Mode.*—Truss the fowl as for boiling, and put it into a stewpan with sufficient clear well-skimmed mutton broth to cover it; add the onion, mace, and a seasoning of pepper and salt; stew very gently for about 1 hour, should the fowl be large, and about ½ hour before it is ready put in the rice, which should be well washed and soaked. When the latter is tender, strain it from the liquor, and put it on a sieve reversed to dry before the fire, and, in the mean time, keep the fowl hot. Dish it, put the rice round as a border, pour a little parsley and butter over the fowl, and the remainder send to table in a tureen. *Time.*—A large fowl, 1 hour. *Average cost*, 2*s*. 6*d*. *Sufficient* for 3 or 4 persons. *Seasonable* all the year.

## FOWLS, to Bone, for Fricassees, Curries, and Pies.

First carve them entirely into joints, then remove the bones, beginning with the legs and wings, at the head of the largest bone; hold this with the fingers, and work the knife as directed in the recipe above. The remainder of the birds is too easily done to require any instructions.

### FOWL, Croquettes of (an Entrée).

*Ingredients.*—3 or 4 shalots, 1 oz. of butter, 1 teaspoonful of flour, white sauce; pepper, salt, and pounded mace to taste; ½ teaspoonful of pounded sugar, the remains of cold roast fowls, the yolks of 2 eggs, egg, and bread-crumbs. *Mode.*—Mince the fowl, carefully removing all skin and bone, and fry the shalots in the butter; add the minced fowl, dredge in the flour, put in the pepper, salt, mace, pounded sugar, and sufficient white sauce to moisten it; stir to it the yolks of 2 well-beaten eggs, and set it by to cool. Then make the mixture up into balls, egg and bread-crumb them, and fry a nice brown. They may be served on a border of mashed potatoes, with gravy or sauce in the centre. *Time.*—10 minutes to fry the balls. *Seasonable* at any time.

### FOWL AND RICE, Croquettes of (an Entrée).

*Ingredients.*—¼ lb. of rice, 1 quart of stock or broth, 3 oz. of butter, minced fowl, egg, and bread-crumbs. *Mode.*—Put the rice into the above proportion of cold stock or broth, and let it boil very gently for ½ hour; then add the butter, and simmer it till quite dry and soft. When cold, make it into balls, hollow out the inside, and fill with minced fowl made by recipe. The mince should be rather thick. Cover over with rice, dip the balls into egg, sprinkle them with bread-crumbs, and fry a nice brown. Dish them, and garnish with fried parsley. Oysters, white sauce, or a little cream, may be stirred into the rice before it cools. *Time.*—½ hour to boil the rice, 10 minutes to fry the croquettes. *Average cost,* exclusive of the fowl, 8*d*. *Seasonable* at any time.

### FOWL, Curried.

*Ingredients.*—1 fowl, 2 oz. of butter, 3 onions sliced, 1 pint of white veal gravy, 1 tablespoonful of curry-powder, 1 tablespoonful of flour, 1 apple, 4 tablespoonfuls of cream, 1 tablespoonful of lemon-juice. *Mode.*—Put the butter into a stewpan, with the onions sliced, the fowl cut into small joints; and the apple peeled, cored, and minced. Fry of a pale brown, add the stock, and stew gently for 20 minutes; rub down the curry-powder and flour with a little of the gravy, quite smoothly, and stir this to the other ingredients; simmer for rather more than ½ hour, and just before serving, add the above proportion of hot cream and lemon-juice. Serve with boiled rice, which may either be heaped lightly on a dish by itself, or put round the curry as a border. *Time.*—50 minutes. *Average cost*, 3*s*. 3*d*. *Sufficient* for 3 or 4 persons. *Seasonable* in the winter.

*Note.*—This curry may be made of cold chicken, but undressed meat will be found far superior.

## FOWL, Fricasseed.

[COLD MEAT COOKERY.] *Ingredients.*—The remains of cold roast fowl, 1 strip of lemon-peel, 1 blade of pounded mace, 1 bunch of savoury herbs, 1 onion, pepper and salt to taste, 1 pint of water, 1 teaspoonful of flour, ¼ pint of cream, the yolks of 2 eggs. *Mode.*—Carve the fowls into nice joints; make gravy of the trimmings and legs, by stewing them with the lemon-peel, mace, herbs, onion, seasoning, and water, until reduced to ½ pint; then strain, and put in the fowl. Warm it through, and thicken with a teaspoonful of flour; stir the yolks of the eggs into the cream; add these to the sauce, let it get thoroughly hot, but do not allow it to boil, or it will curdle. *Time.*—1 hour to make the gravy, ¼ hour to warm the fowl. *Average cost*, exclusive of the cold chicken, 8*d*. *Seasonable* at any time.

## FOWLS, Fried.

[COLD MEAT COOKERY.] *Ingredients.*—The remains of cold roast fowls, vinegar, salt and cayenne to taste, 3 or 4 minced shalots. For the batter,—½ lb. of flour, ½ pint of hot water, 2 oz. of butter, the whites of 2 eggs. *Mode.*—Cut the fowl into nice joints; steep them for an hour in a little vinegar, with salt, cayenne, and minced shalots. Make the batter by mixing the flour and water smoothly together; melt in it the butter, and add the whites of egg beaten to a froth; take out the pieces of fowl, dip them in the batter, and fry in boiling lard, a nice brown. Pile them high in the dish, and garnish with fried parsley or rolled bacon. When approved, a sauce or gravy may be served with them. *Time.*—10 minutes to fry the fowl. *Average cost*, exclusive of the cold fowl, 8*d*. *Seasonable* at any time.

## FOWLS, Fried.

[Cold Meat Cookery.] *Ingredients.*—The remains of cold roast fowl, vinegar, salt and cayenne to taste, 4 minced shalots, yolk of egg; to every teacupful of bread-crumbs allow 1 blade of pounded mace, ½ teaspoonful of minced lemon-peel, 1 saltspoonful of salt, a few grains of cayenne. *Mode.*—Steep the pieces of fowl as in the preceding recipe, then dip them into the yolk of an egg or clarified butter; sprinkle over bread-crumbs with which have been mixed salt, mace, cayenne, and lemon-peel in the above proportion. Fry a light brown, and serve with or without gravy, as may be preferred. *Time.*—10 minutes to fry the fowl. *Average cost*, exclusive of the cold fowl, 6*d*. *Seasonable* at any time.

## FOWLS, Fried, and French Beans.

[Cold Meat Cookery.] *Ingredients.*—The remains of cold roast fowl; the yolk of 1 egg, 2 oz. of butter, 1 blade of pounded mace, ¼ saltspoonful of grated nutmeg, bread-crumbs and chopped parsley. *Mode.*—Cut the fowl into neat joints, brush them over with the yolk of egg, and sprinkle them with bread-crumbs, with which the *parsley, nutmeg,* and *mace* have been well mixed. Fry the fowl in the butter until of a nice brown, and dish the pieces on French beans boiled, and afterwards simmered for a minute or two in butter. The dish should be garnished with rolled bacon. *Time.*—10 minutes to fry the fowl. *Average cost*, exclusive of the cold fowl, 6*d*. *Seasonable* from July to September.

## FOWL au Gratin.

[Cold Meat Cookery.] *Ingredients.*—The remains of either cold roast or boiled fowl, ½ pint of Béchamel sauce, a dessertspoonful of grated Parmesan cheese, pepper and salt to taste, ¼ saltspoonful of grated nutmeg, ¼ pint of cream, 2 tablespoonfuls of bread-crumbs, fried potatoes. *Mode.*—Mince the fowl not too finely, and make it hot in the Béchamel sauce, to which the nutmeg, pepper and salt, and cream, have been added. When well mixed, serve the fowl on to a dish, cover it with the bread-crumbs and Parmesan cheese, drop over a little clarified butter, and bake in the oven until of a pale brown. Garnish the dish with fried potatoes. *Time.*—10 minutes to warm the fowl, 10 minutes to bake. *Seasonable* at any time.

## FOWL, Hashed. An Entrée.

[Cold Meat Cookery.] *Ingredients.*—The remains of cold roast fowl, 1 pint of water, 1 onion, 2 or 3 small carrots, 1 blade of pounded mace, pepper and salt to taste, 1 small bunch of savoury herbs, thickening of butter and flour, 1½ tablespoonful of mushroom ketchup. *Mode.*—Cut off the best joints from the fowl, and the remainder make into gravy, by adding to the bones and trimmings a pint of water, an onion sliced and fried of a nice brown, the carrots, mace, seasoning, and herbs. Let these stew gently for 1½ hour, strain the liquor, and thicken with a little flour and butter. Lay in the fowl, thoroughly warm it through, add the ketchup, and garnish with sippets of toasted bread. *Time.*—Altogether 1¾ hour. *Average cost*, exclusive of the cold fowl, 4*d*. *Seasonable* at any time.

## FOWL, Hashed, Indian Fashion (an Entrée).

[Cold Meat Cookery.] *Ingredients.*—The remains of cold roast fowl, 3 or 4 sliced onions, 1 apple, 2 oz. of butter, pounded mace, pepper and salt to taste, 1 tablespoonful of curry-powder, 2 tablespoonfuls of vinegar, 1 tablespoonful of flour, 1 teaspoonful of pounded sugar, 1 pint of gravy. *Mode.*—Cut the onions into slices, mince the apple, and fry these in the butter; add pounded mace, pepper, salt, curry-powder, vinegar, flour, and sugar in the above proportions; when the onion is brown, put in the gravy, which should be previously made from the bones and trimmings of the fowls, and stew for ¾ hour; add the fowl cut into nice-sized joints, let it warm through, and when quite tender, serve. The dish should be garnished with an edging of boiled rice. *Time.*—1 hour. *Average cost*, exclusive of the fowl, 8*d*. *Seasonable* at any time.

## FOWL, an Indian Dish of (an Entrée).

[Cold Meat Cookery.] *Ingredients.*—The remains of cold roast fowl, 3 or 4 sliced onions, 1 tablespoonful of curry-powder, salt to taste. *Mode.*—Divide the fowl into joints; slice and fry the onions in a little butter, taking care not to burn them; sprinkle over the fowl a little curry-powder and salt; fry these nicely, pile them high in the centre of the dish, cover with the onion, and serve with a cut lemon on a plate. Care must be taken that the onions are not greasy: they should be quite dry, but not burnt. *Time.*—5 minutes to fry the onions, 10 minutes to fry the fowl. *Average cost*, exclusive of the fowl, 4d. *Seasonable* during the winter months.

## FOWL à la Mayonnaise.

*Ingredients.*—A cold roast fowl, Mayonnaise sauce, 4 or 5 young lettuces, 4 hard-boiled eggs, a few water-cresses, endive. *Mode.*—Cut the fowl into neat joints, lay them in a deep dish, piling them high in the centre, sauce the fowl with Mayonnaise, and garnish the dish with young lettuces cut in halves, water-cresses, endive, and hard-boiled eggs: these may be sliced in rings, or laid on the dish whole, cutting off at the bottom a piece of the white, to make the egg stand. All kinds of cold meat and solid fish may be dressed à la Mayonnaise, and make excellent luncheon or supper dishes. The sauce should not be poured over the fowls until the moment of serving. Should a very large Mayonnaise be required, use 2 fowls instead of one, with an equal proportion of the remaining ingredients. *Average cost*, with one fowl, 3s. 6d. *Sufficient* for a moderate-sized dish. *Seasonable* from April to September.

## FOWL, Minced (an Entrée).

[COLD MEAT COOKERY.] *Ingredients.*—The remains of cold roast fowl, 2 hard-boiled eggs, salt, cayenne, and pounded mace, 1 onion, 1 faggot of savoury herbs, 6 tablespoonfuls of cream, 1 oz. of butter, two teaspoonfuls of flour, ½ teaspoonful of finely-minced lemon-peel, 1 tablespoonful of lemon-juice. *Mode.*—Cut out from the fowl all the white meat, and mince it finely without any skin or bone; put the bones, skin, and trimmings into a stewpan with an onion, a bunch of savoury herbs, a blade of mace, and nearly a pint of water; let this stew for an hour, then strain the liquor. Chop the eggs small; mix them with the fowl; add salt, cayenne, and pounded mace, put in the gravy and remaining ingredients; let the whole just boil, and serve with sippets of toasted bread. *Time.*—Rather more than 1 hour. *Average cost*, exclusive of the fowl, 8d. *Seasonable* at any time.

*Note.*—Another way to make this is to mince the fowl, and warm it in white sauce or Béchamel. When dressed like this, 3 or 4 poached eggs may be placed on the top: oysters, or chopped mushrooms, or balls of oyster forcemeat, may be laid round the dish.

## FOWL, Minced, à la Béchamel.

[Cold Meat Cookery.] *Ingredients.*—The remains of cold roast fowl, 6 tablespoonfuls of Béchamel sauce, 6 tablespoonfuls of white stock, the white of 1 egg, bread-crumbs, clarified butter. *Mode.*—Take the remains of roast fowls, mince the white meat very small, and put it into a stewpan with the Béchamel and stock; stir it well over the fire, and just let it boil up. Pour the mince into a dish, beat up the white of egg, spread it over, and strew on it a few grated bread-crumbs; pour a very little clarified butter on the whole, and brown either before the fire or with a salamander. This should be served in a silver dish, if at hand. *Time.*—2 or 3 minutes to simmer in the sauce. *Seasonable* at any time.

## FOWL, Ragoût of.

[Cold Meat Cookery.] *Ingredients.*—The remains of cold roast fowls, 3 shalots, 2 blades of mace, a faggot of savoury herbs, 2 or 3 slices of lean ham, 1 pint of stock or water, pepper and salt to taste, 1 onion, 1 dessertspoonful of flour, 1 tablespoonful of lemon-juice, ½ teaspoonful of pounded sugar, 1 oz. of butter. *Mode.*—Cut the fowls up into neat pieces, the same as for a fricassee; put the trimmings into a stewpan with the shalots, mace, herbs, ham, onion, and stock (water may be substituted for this). Boil it slowly for 1 hour, strain the liquor, and put a small piece of butter into a stewpan; when melted, dredge in sufficient flour to dry up the butter, and stir it over the fire. Put in the strained liquor, boil for a few minutes, and strain it again over the pieces of fowl. Squeeze in the lemon-juice, add the sugar and a seasoning of pepper and salt, make it hot, but do not allow it to boil; lay the fowl neatly on the dish, and garnish with croûtons. *Time.*—Altogether 1½ hour. *Average cost*, exclusive of the cold fowl, 9*d*. *Seasonable* at any time.

## FOWLS, Roast.

*Ingredients.*—A pair of fowls, a little flour. *Mode.*—Fowls, to be tender, should be killed a couple of days before they are dressed; when the feathers come out easily; then let them be picked and cooked. In drawing them be careful not to break the gall-bag, as, wherever it touches, it would impart a very bitter taste; the liver and gizzard should also be preserved. Truss them in the following manner:—After having carefully picked them, cut off the head, and skewer the skin of the neck down over the back. Cut off the claws, dip the legs in boiling water, and scrape them; turn the pinions under, run a skewer through them and the middle of the legs, which should be passed through the body to the pinion and leg on the other side, one skewer securing the limbs on both sides. The liver and gizzard should be placed in the wings, the liver on one side and the gizzard on the other. Tie the legs together by passing a trussing-needle, threaded with twine, through the backbone, and secure it on the other side. If trussed like a capon, the legs are placed more apart. When firmly trussed, singe them all over; put them down to a bright clear fire, paper the breasts with a sheet of buttered paper, and keep the fowls well basted. Roast them for ¾ hour, more or less, according to the size, and 10 minutes before serving, remove the paper, dredge the fowls with a little fine flour, put a piece of butter into the basting-ladle, and as it melts baste the fowls with it; when nicely frothed and of a rich colour, serve with good brown gravy (a little of which should be poured over the fowls), and a tureen of well-made bread sauce. Mushroom, oyster, or egg sauce, are very suitable accompaniments to roast fowl.—Chicken is roasted in the same manner. *Time.*—A very large fowl, quite 1 hour; a medium-sized one, ¾ hour; chicken, ½ hour, or rather longer. *Average cost*, in full season, 5*s.* a pair; when scarce, 7*s.* 6*d.* the pair. *Sufficient* for 6 or 7 persons. *Seasonable* all the year, but scarce in early spring.

**ROAST FOWL.**

## FOWL, Roast, to Carve.

A roast fowl is carved in the same manner as a boiled fowl, viz., by cutting along the line from 1 to 2, and then round the leg between it and the wing. The markings and detached pieces, as shown in the engravings under the heading of "Boiled Fowl," supersede the necessity of our lengthily again describing the operation. It may be added, that the liver, being considered a delicacy, should be divided, and one half served with each wing. In the case of a fowl being stuffed, it will be proper to give each guest a portion, unless it be not agreeable to some one of the party.

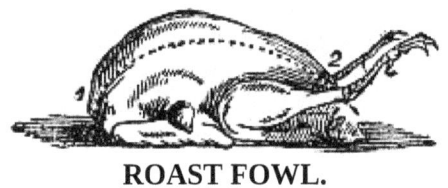
ROAST FOWL.

## FOWL, Roast, Stuffed.

*Ingredients.*—A large fowl, forcemeat, a little flour. *Mode.*—Select a large plump fowl, fill the breast with forcemeat, truss it firmly, the same as for a plain roast fowl, dredge it with flour, and put it down to a bright fire. Roast it for nearly or quite an hour, should it be very large; remove the skewers, and serve with a good brown gravy and a tureen of bread sauce. *Time.*—Large fowl, nearly or quite 1 hour. *Average cost*, in full season, 2s. 6d. each. *Sufficient* for 4 or 5 persons. *Seasonable* all the year, but scarce in early spring.

*Note.*—Sausage-meat stuffing may be substituted: this is now a very general mode of serving fowl.

## FOWL SAUTE with Peas (an Entrée).

[Cold Meat Cookery.] *Ingredients.*—The remains of cold roast fowl, 2 oz. of butter, pepper, salt, and pounded mace to taste, 1 dessertspoonful of flour, ½ pint of weak stock, 1 pint of green peas, 1 teaspoonful of pounded sugar. *Mode.*—Cut the fowl into nice pieces; put the butter into a stewpan; sautez or fry the fowl a nice brown colour, previously sprinkling it with pepper, salt, and pounded mace. Dredge in the flour, shake the ingredients well round, then add the stock and peas, and stew till the latter are tender, which will be in about 20 minutes; put in the pounded sugar, and serve, placing the chicken round, and the peas in the middle of the dish. When liked, mushrooms may be substituted for the peas. *Time.*—Altogether 40 minutes. *Average cost*, exclusive of the fowl, 7d. *Seasonable* from June to August.

## FOWL SCOLLOPS.

[COLD MEAT COOKERY.] *Ingredients.*—The remains of cold roast or boiled fowl, ½ pint of Béchamel, or white sauce. *Mode.*—Strip off the skin from the fowl; cut the meat into thin slices, and warm them in about ½ pint, or rather more, of Béchamel, or white sauce. When quite hot, serve, and garnish the dish with rolled ham or bacon toasted. *Time.*—1 minute to simmer the slices of fowl. *Seasonable* at any time.

## FRENCH TERMS used in modern Household Cookery, explained.

ASPIC.—A savoury jelly, used as an exterior moulding for cold game, poultry, fish, &c. This, being of a transparent nature, allows the article which it covers to be seen through it. This may also be used for decorating or garnishing.

ASSIETTE (plate).—*Assiettes* are the small *entrées* and *hors-d'œuvres*, the quantity of which does not exceed what a plate will hold. At dessert, fruits, cheese, chestnuts, biscuits, &c., if served upon a plate, are termed *assiettes*.—ASSIETTE VOLANTE is a dish which a servant hands round to the guests, but is not placed upon the table. Small cheese soufflés and different dishes, which ought to be served very hot, are frequently made *assiettes volantes*.

AU-BLEU.—Fish dressed in such a manner as to have a *bluish* appearance.

BAIN-MARIE.—An open saucepan or kettle of nearly boiling water, in which a smaller vessel can be set for cooking and warming. This is very useful for keeping articles hot, without altering their quantity or quality. If you keep sauce, broth, or soup by the fireside, the soup reduces and becomes too strong, and the sauce thickens as well as reduces; but this is prevented by using the *bain-marie*, in which the water should be very hot, but not boiling.

BÉCHAMEL.—French white sauce, now frequently used in English cookery.

BLANCH.—To whiten poultry, vegetables, fruit, &c., by plunging them into boiling water for a short time, and afterwards plunging them into cold water, there to remain until they are cold.

BLANQUETTE.—A sort of fricassee.

BOUILLI.—Beef or other meat boiled; but, generally speaking, boiled beef is understood by the term.

BOUILLIE.—A French dish resembling hasty-pudding.

BOUILLON.—A thin broth or soup.

BRAISE.—To stew meat with fat bacon until it is tender, it having previously been blanched.

BRAISIÈRE.—A saucepan having a lid with ledges, to put fire on the top.

BRIDER.—To pass a packthread through poultry, game, &c., to keep together their members.

CARAMEL (burnt sugar).—This is made with a piece of sugar, of the size of a nut, browned in the bottom of a saucepan; upon which a cupful of stock is gradually poured, stirring all the time, and adding the broth little by little. It may be used with the feather of a quill, to colour meats, such as the upper part of fricandeaux; and to impart colour to sauces. Caramel made with water instead of stock may be used to colour *compôtes* and other *entremets*.

CASSEROLE.—A crust of rice, which, after having been moulded into the form of a pie, is baked, and then filled with a fricassee of white meat or a purée of game.

COMPÔTE.—A stew, as of fruit or pigeons.

CONSOMMÉ.—Rich stock, or gravy.

CROQUETTE.—Ball of fried rice or potatoes.

CROÛTONS.—Sippets of bread.

DAUBIÈRE.—An oval stewpan, in which *daubes* are cooked; *daubes* being meat or fowl stewed in sauce.

DÉSOSSER.—To *bone,* or take out the bones from poultry, game, or fish. This is an operation requiring considerable experience.

Entrées.—Small side or corner dishes served with the first course.

Entremets.—Small side or corner dishes served with the second course.

Escalopes.—Collops; small, round, thin pieces of tender meat, or of fish, beaten with the handle of a strong knife to make them tender.

Feuilletage.—Puff-paste.

Flamber.—To singe fowl or game, after they have been picked.

Foncer.—To put in the bottom of a saucepan slices of ham, veal, or thin broad slices of bacon.

Galette.—A broad thin cake.

Gâteau.—A cake, correctly speaking; but used sometimes to denote a pudding and a kind of tart.

Glacer.—To glaze, or spread upon hot meats, or larded fowl, a thick and rich sauce or gravy, called *glaze*. This is laid on with a feather or brush, and in confectionary the term means to ice fruits and pastry with sugar, which glistens on hardening.

Hors-d'œvres.—Small dishes, or *assiettes volantes* of sardines, anchovies, and other relishes of this kind, served to the guests during the first course. (*See* Assiettes volantes.)

Lit.—A bed or layer; articles in thin slices are placed in layers, other articles, or seasoning, being laid between them.

Maigre.—Broth, soup, or gravy, made without meat.

Matelote.—A rich fish-stew, which is generally composed of carp, eels, trout, or barbel. It is made with wine.

Mayonnaise.—Cold sauce, or salad dressing.

Menu.—The bill of fare.

Meringue.—A kind of icing, made of whites of eggs and sugar, well beaten.

MIROTON.—Larger slices of meat than collops; such as slices of beef for a vinaigrette, or ragoût or stew of onions.

MOUILLER.—To add water, broth, or other liquid, during the cooking.

PANER.—To cover with very fine crumbs of bread, meats, or any other articles to be cooked on the gridiron, in the oven, or frying-pan.

PIQUER.—To lard with strips of fat bacon, poultry, game, meat, &c. This should always be done according to the vein of the meat, so that in carving you slice the bacon across as well as the meat.

POELÉE.—Stock used instead of water for boiling turkeys, sweetbreads, fowls, and vegetables, to render them less insipid.—This is rather an expensive preparation.

PURÉE.—Vegetables or meat reduced to a very smooth pulp, which is afterwards mixed with enough liquid to make it of the consistency of very thick soup.

RAGOÛT.—Stew or hash.

REMOULADE.—Salad dressing.

RISSOLES.—Pastry, made of light puff-paste, and cut into various forms, and fried. They may be filled with fish, meat, or sweets.

ROUX.—Brown and white; French thickening.

SALMI.—Ragoût of game previously roasted.

SAUCE PIQUANTE.—A sharp sauce, in which somewhat of a vinegar flavour predominates.

SAUTER.—To dress with sauce in a saucepan, repeatedly moving it about.

TAMIS.—Tammy, a sort of open cloth or sieve through which to strain broth and sauces, so as to rid them of small bones, froth, &c.

TOURTE.—Tart. Fruit pie.

TROUSSER.—To truss a bird; to put together the body and tie the wings and thighs, in order to round it for roasting or boiling, each being tied then with packthread, to keep it in the required form.

VOL-AU-VENT.—A rich crust of very fine puff-paste, which may be filled with various delicate ragoûts or fricassees, of fish, flesh, or fowl. Fruit may also be inclosed in a *vol-au-vent*.

## FRITTERS, Indian.

*Ingredients.*—3 tablespoonfuls of flour, boiling water, the yolks of 4 eggs, the whites of 2, hot lard or clarified dripping, jam. *Mode.*—Put the flour into a basin, and pour over it sufficient *boiling* water to make it into a stiff paste, taking care to stir and beat it well, to prevent it getting lumpy. Leave it a little time to cool, and then break into it (*without beating them at first*) the yolks of 4 eggs and the whites of 2, and stir and beat all well together. Have ready some boiling lard or butter; drop a dessertspoonful of batter in at a time, and fry the fritters of a light brown. They should rise so much as to be almost like balls. Serve on a dish, with a spoonful of preserve or marmalade dropped in between each fritter. This is an excellent dish for a hasty addition to dinner, if a guest unexpectedly arrives, it being so easily and quickly made, and it is always a great favourite. *Time.*—From 5 to 8 minutes to fry the fritters. *Average cost*, exclusive of the jam, 5*d*. *Sufficient* for 4 or 5 persons. *Seasonable* at any time.

## FRITTERS, Plain.

*Ingredients.*—3 oz. of flour, 3 eggs, 1/3 pint of milk. *Mode.*—Mix the flour to a smooth batter with a small quantity of the milk; stir in the eggs, which should be well whisked, and then the remainder of the milk; beat the whole to a perfectly smooth batter, and should it be found not quite thin enough, add two or three tablespoonfuls more milk. Have ready a frying-pan, with plenty of boiling lard in it; drop in rather more than a tablespoonful at a time of the batter and fry the fritters a nice brown, turning them when sufficiently cooked on one side. Drain them well from the greasy moisture by placing them upon a piece of blotting-paper before the fire; dish them on a white d'oyley, sprinkle over them sifted sugar, and send to table with them a cut lemon and plenty of pounded sugar. *Time.*—From 6 to 8 minutes. *Average cost*, 4*d*. *Sufficient* for 3 or 4 persons. *Seasonable* at any time.

## FRUIT, to Bottle Fresh. (Very useful in Winter.)

*Ingredients.*—Fresh fruits, such as currants, raspberries, cherries, gooseberries, plums of all kinds, damsons, &c.; wide-mouthed glass bottles, new corks to fit them tightly. *Mode.*—Let the fruit be full grown, but not too ripe, and gathered in dry weather. Pick it off the stalks without bruising or breaking the skin, and reject any that is at all blemished: if gathered in the damp, or if the skins are cut at all, the fruit will mould. Have ready some *perfectly dry* glass bottles, and some nice *new* soft corks or bungs; burn a match in each bottle, to exhaust the air, and quickly place the fruit in to be preserved; gently cork the bottles, and put them in a very cool oven, where let them remain until the fruit has shrunk away a fourth part. Then take the bottles out; *do not open them*, but immediately beat the corks in tight, cut off the tops, and cover them with melted resin. If kept in a dry place, the fruit will remain good for months; and on this principally depends the success of the preparation; for if stored away in a place that is in the least damp, the fruit will soon spoil. *Time.*—From 5 to 6 hours in a very slow oven.

## FRUIT, to Bottle Fresh.

*Ingredients.*—Any kind of fresh fruit, such as currants, cherries, gooseberries, all kinds of plums, &c.; wide-mouthed glass bottles, new corks to fit them tightly. *Mode.*—the fruit must be full-grown, not too ripe, and gathered on a fine day. Let it be carefully picked and put into the bottles, which must be clean and perfectly dry. Tie over the tops of the bottles pieces of bladder; stand the bottles in a large pot, copper, or boiler, with cold water to reach to their necks; kindle a fire under, let the water boil, and as the bladders begin to rise and puff, prick them. As soon as the water boils, extinguish the fire, and let the bottles remain where they are, to become cold. The next day remove the bladders, and strew over the fruit a thick layer of pounded sugar; fit the bottles with cork, and let each cork lie close at hand to its own bottle. Hold for a few moments, in the neck of the bottle, two or three lighted matches, and when they have filled the bottle neck with gas, and before they go out, remove them very quickly; instantly cork the bottle closely, and dip it in bottle-cement. *Time.*—Altogether about 8 hours.

## FRUIT, to Bottle Fresh, with Sugar. (Very useful in Winter.)

*Ingredients.*—Any kind of fresh fruit; to each quart bottle allow ¼ lb. of pounded sugar. *Mode.*—Let the fruit be gathered in dry weather. Pick it carefully, and drop it into *clean* and *very dry* quart glass bottles, sprinkling over it the above proportion of pounded sugar to each quart. Put the corks in the bottles, and place them in a copper of cold water up to their necks, with small hay-wisps round them, to prevent the bottles from knocking together. Light the fire under, bring the water gradually to boil, and let it simmer gently until the fruit in the bottles is reduced nearly one third. Extinguish the fire, *and let the bottles remain in the water until it is perfectly cold*; then take them out, make the corks secure, and cover them with melted resin or wax. *Time.*—About ½ hour from the time the water commences to boil.

## FRUIT TURNOVERS (suitable for Pic-Nics).

*Ingredients.*—Puff-paste, any kind of fruit, sugar to taste. *Mode.*—Make some puff-paste by recipe; roll it out to the thickness of about ¼ inch, and cut it out in pieces of a circular form; pile the fruit on half of the paste, sprinkle over some sugar, wet the edges and turn the paste over. Press the edges together, ornament them, and brush the turnovers over with the white of an egg; sprinkle over sifted sugar, and bake on tins, in a brisk oven, for about 20 minutes. Instead of putting the fruit in raw, it may be boiled down with a little sugar first, and then inclosed in the crust; or jam, of any kind, may be substituted for fresh fruit. *Time.*—20 minutes. *Sufficient.*—½ lb. of puff-paste will make a dozen turnovers. *Seasonable* at any time.

## GAME, Hashed.

[COLD MEAT COOKERY.] *Ingredients.*—The remains of cold game, 1 onion stuck with 3 cloves, a few whole peppers, a strip of lemon-peel, salt to taste, thickening of butter and flour, 1 glass of port wine, 1 tablespoonful of lemon-juice, 1 tablespoonful of ketchup, 1 pint of water or weak stock. *Mode.*—Cut the remains of cold game into joints, reserve the best pieces, and the inferior ones and trimmings put into a stewpan with the onion, pepper, lemon-peel, salt, and water or weak stock; stew these for about an hour, and strain the gravy; thicken it with butter and flour; add the wine, lemon-juice, and ketchup; lay in the pieces of game, and let them gradually warm through by the side of the fire; do not allow it to boil, or the game will be hard. When on the point of simmering, serve, and garnish the dish with sippets of toasted bread. *Time.*—Altogether 1¼ hour. *Seasonable* from August to March.

*Note.*—Any kind of game may be hashed by the above recipe, and the flavour may be varied by adding flavoured vinegars, curry powder, &c.; but we cannot recommend these latter ingredients, as a dish of game should really have a gamy taste; and if too many sauces, essences, &c., are added to the gravy, they quite overpower and destroy the flavour the dish should possess.

## GERMAN PUFFS.

*Ingredients.*—2 oz. of flour, 2 eggs, ½ pint of new milk, 2 oz. of melted butter, little salt and nutmeg. *Mode.*—Let the 2 eggs be well beaten, then mix all the ingredients well together, and heat them up just before they are put into little cups half full for baking. Bake for ¼ hour in a hot oven till the puffs are of a nice brown; turn out on a flat dish, rub a little butter over each puff, and dust on it powdered sugar. *Time.*—¼ hour. *Average cost*, 6d. *Seasonable* at any time.

## GHERKINS, Pickled.

*Ingredients.*—Salt and water, 1 oz. of bruised ginger ½ oz. of whole black pepper, ¼ oz. of whole allspice, 4 cloves, 2 blades of mace, a little horseradish. This proportion of pepper, spices, &c., for 1 quart of vinegar. *Mode.*—Let the gherkins remain in salt and water for 3 or 4 days, when take them out, wipe perfectly dry, and put them into a stone jar. Boil sufficient vinegar to cover them, with spices and pepper, &c., in the above proportion, for 10 minutes; pour it, quite boiling, over the gherkins, cover the jar with vine-leaves, and put over them a plate, setting them near the fire, where they must remain all night. Next day drain off the vinegar, boil it up again, and pour it hot over them. Cover up with fresh leaves, and let the whole remain till quite cold. Now tie down closely with bladder to exclude the air, and in a month or two they will be fit for use. *Time.*—4 days. *Seasonable* from the middle of July to the end of August.

## GIBLET PIE.

*Ingredients.*—A set of duck or goose giblets, 1 lb. of rump-steak, 1 onion, ½ teaspoonful of whole black pepper, a bunch of savoury herbs, plain crust. *Mode.*—Clean, and put the giblets into a stewpan with an onion, whole pepper, and a bunch of savoury herbs; add rather more than a pint of water, and simmer gently for about 1½ hour. Take them out, let them cool, and cut them into pieces; line the bottom of a pie-dish with a few pieces of rump-steak; add a layer of giblets and a few more pieces of steak; season with pepper and salt, and pour in the gravy (which should be strained), that the giblets were stewed in; cover with a plain crust, and bake for rather more than 1½ hour in a brisk oven. Cover a piece of paper over the pie, to prevent the crust taking too much colour. *Time.*—1½ hour to stew the giblets, about 1 hour to bake the pie. *Average cost*, exclusive of the giblets, 1*s.* 4*d. Sufficient* for 5 or 6 persons.

## GIBLET SOUP.

*Ingredients.*—3 sets of goose or duck giblets, 2 lbs. of shin of beef, a few bones, 1 ox-tail, 2 mutton-shanks, 2 large onions, 2 carrots, 1 large faggot of herbs, salt and pepper to taste, ¼ pint of cream, 1 oz. of butter mixed with a dessertspoonful of flour, 3 quarts of water. *Mode.*—Scald the giblets, cut the gizzards in 8 pieces, and put them in a stewpan with the beef, bones, ox-tail, mutton-shanks, onions, herbs, pepper, and salt; add the 3 quarts of water, and simmer till the giblets are tender, taking care to skim well. When the giblets are done, take them out, put them in your tureen, strain the soup through a sieve, add the cream and butter, mixed with a dessertspoonful of flour, boil it up for a few minutes, and pour it over the giblets. It can be flavoured with port wine and a little mushroom ketchup, instead of cream. Add salt to taste. *Time.*—3 hours. *Average cost*, 9*d.* per quart. *Seasonable* all the year. *Sufficient* for 10 persons.

## GINGER, Apple. (A Dessert Dish.)

*Ingredients.*—2 lbs. of any kind of hard apples, 2 lbs. of loaf sugar, 1½ pint of water, 1 oz. of tincture of ginger. *Mode.*—Boil the sugar and water until they form a rich syrup, adding the ginger when it boils up. Pare, core, and cut the apples into pieces; dip them in cold water to preserve the colour, and boil them in the syrup until transparent; but be careful not to let them break. Put the pieces of apple into jars, pour over the syrup, and carefully exclude the air, by well covering them. It will remain good some time, if kept in a dry place. *Time.*—From 5 to 10 minutes to boil the syrup; about ½ hour to simmer the apples. *Average cost,* 2*s*. *Sufficient* for 7 or 8 persons. *Seasonable.*—Make this in September, October, or November.

## GINGER-BEER.

*Ingredients.*—2½ lbs. of loaf sugar, 1½ oz. of bruised ginger, 1 oz. of cream of tartar, the rind and juice of 2 lemons, 3 gallons of boiling water, two large tablespoonfuls of thick and fresh brewer's yeast. *Mode.*—Peel the lemons, squeeze the juice, strain it, and put the peel and juice into a large earthen pan, with the bruised ginger, cream of tartar, and loaf sugar. Put over these ingredients 3 gallons of *boiling* water; let it stand until just warm, when add the yeast, which should be thick and perfectly fresh. Stir the contents of the pan well, and let them remain near the fire all night, covering the pan over with a cloth. The next day skim off the yeast, and pour the liquor carefully into another vessel, leaving the sediment; then bottle immediately, and tie the corks down, and in 3 days the ginger-beer will be fit for use. For some tastes, the above proportion of sugar may be found rather too large, when it may be diminished; but the beer will not keep so long good. *Average cost* for this quantity, 2*s*.; or ½*d*. per bottle. *Sufficient* to fill 4 dozen ginger-beer bottles. *Seasonable.*—This should be made during the summer months.

## GINGER CREAM.

*Ingredients.*—The yolks of 4 eggs, 1 pint of cream, 3 oz. of preserved ginger, 2 dessertspoonfuls of syrup, sifted sugar to taste, 1 oz. of isinglass. *Mode.*—Slice the ginger finely; put it into a basin with the syrup, the well-beaten yolks of eggs, and the cream; mix these ingredients well together, and stir them over the fire for about 10 minutes, or until the mixture thickens; then take it off the fire, whisk till nearly cold, sweeten to taste, add the isinglass, which should be melted and strained, and serve the cream in a glass dish. It may be garnished with slices of preserved ginger or candied citron. *Time.*—About 10 minutes to stir the cream over the fire. *Average cost*, with cream at 1*s.* per pint, 3*s.* 6*d.* *Sufficient* for a good-sized dish. *Seasonable* at any time.

## GINGER, Preserved,

Comes from the West Indies. It is made by scalding the roots when they are green and full of sap, then peeling them in cold water and putting them into jars, with a rich syrup; in which state we receive them. It should be chosen of a deep yellow colour, with a little transparency. What is dark-coloured, fibrous, and stringy, is not good. Ginger roots, fit for preserving and in size equal to West Indian, have been produced in the Royal Agricultural Garden in Edinburgh.

## GINGER PUDDING.

*Ingredients.*—½ lb. of flour, ¼ lb. of suet, ¼ lb. of moist sugar, 2 large teaspoonfuls of grated ginger. *Mode.*—Shred the suet very fine, mix it with the flour, sugar, and ginger; stir all well together; butter a basin, and put the mixture in dry; tie a cloth over, and boil for 3 hours. *Time.*—3 hours. *Average cost*, 6*d.* *Sufficient* for 5 or 6 persons. *Seasonable* at any time.

## GINGER WINE.

*Ingredients.*—To 9 gallons of water allow 27 lbs. of loaf sugar, 9 lemons, 12 oz. of bruised ginger, 3 tablespoonfuls of yeast, 2 lbs. of raisins stoned and chopped, 1 pint of brandy. *Mode.*—Boil together for 1 hour in a copper (let it previously be well scoured and beautifully clean) the water, sugar, *lemon-rinds*, and bruised ginger; remove every particle of scum as it rises, and when the liquor is sufficiently boiled, put it into a large tub or pan, as it must not remain in the copper. When nearly cold, add the yeast, which must be thick and very fresh, and, the next day, put all in a dry cask with the strained lemon-juice and chopped raisins. Stir the wine every day for a fortnight; then add the brandy, stop the cask down by degrees, and in a few weeks it will be fit to bottle. *Average cost*, 2*s.* per gallon. *Sufficient* to make 9 gallons of wine. *Seasonable.*—The best time for making this wine is either in March or September.

*Note.*—Wine made early in March will be fit to bottle in June.

## GINGERBREAD, Thick.

*Ingredients.*—1 lb. of treacle, ¼ lb. of butter, ¼ lb. of coarse brown sugar, 1½ lb. of flour, 1 oz. of ginger, ½ oz. of ground allspice, 1 teaspoonful of carbonate of soda, ¼ pint of warm milk, 3 eggs. *Mode.*—Put the flour into a basin, with the sugar, ginger, and allspice; mix these together; warm the butter, and add it, with the treacle, to the other ingredients. Stir well; make the milk just warm, dissolve the carbonate of soda in it, and mix the whole into a nice smooth dough with the eggs, which should be previously well whisked; pour the mixture into a buttered tin, and bake it from ¾ to 1 hour, or longer, should the gingerbread be very thick. Just before it is done, brush the top over with the yolk of an egg beaten up with a little milk, and put it back in the oven to finish baking. *Time.*—¾ to 1 hour. *Average cost*, 1*s*. per square. *Seasonable* at any time.

## GINGERBREAD, White.

*Ingredients.*—1 lb. of flour, ½ lb. of butter, ½ lb. of loaf sugar, the rind of 1 lemon, 1 oz. of ground ginger, 1 nutmeg grated, ½ teaspoonful of carbonate of soda, 1 gill of milk. *Mode.*—Rub the butter into the flour; add the sugar, which should be finely pounded and sifted, and the minced lemon-rind, ginger, and nutmeg. Mix these well together; make the milk just warm, stir in the soda, and work the whole into a nice smooth paste; roll it out, cut it into cakes, and bake in a moderate oven from 15 to 20 minutes. *Time.*—15 to 20 minutes. *Average cost*, 1*s*. 3*d*. *Seasonable* at any time.

## GINGERBREAD-NUTS, Rich Sweetmeats.

*Ingredients.*—1 lb. of treacle, ¼ lb. of clarified butter, 1 lb. of coarse brown sugar, 2 oz. of ground ginger, 1 oz. of candied orange-peel, 1 oz. of candied angelica, ½ oz. of candied lemon-peel, ½ oz. of coriander seeds, ½ oz. of caraway seeds, 1 egg; flour. *Mode.*—Put the treacle into a basin, and pour over it the butter, melted so as not to oil, the sugar, and ginger. Stir these ingredients well together, and whilst mixing, add the candied peel, which should be cut into very small pieces, but not bruised, and the caraway and coriander seeds, which should be pounded. Having mixed all thoroughly together, break in an egg, and work the whole up with as much fine flour as may be necessary to form a paste. Make this into nuts of any size, and put them on a tin plate, and bake in a slow oven from ¼ to ½ hour. *Time.*—¼ to ½ hour. *Average cost,* from 1*s.* to 1*s.* 4*d.* per lb. *Seasonable* at any time.

## GINGERBREAD-NUTS, Sunderland. (An Excellent Recipe.)

*Ingredients.*—1¾ lb. of treacle, 1 lb. of moist sugar, 1 lb. of butter, 2¾ lbs. of flour, 1½ oz. of ground ginger, 1½ oz. of allspice, 1½ oz. of coriander-seeds. *Mode.*—Let the allspice, coriander-seeds, and ginger be freshly ground; put them into a basin, with the flour and sugar, and mix these ingredients well together; warm the treacle and butter together; then with a spoon work it into the flour, &c. until the whole forms a nice smooth paste. Drop the mixture from the spoon on a piece of buttered paper, and bake in rather a slow oven from 20 minutes to ½ hour. A little candied lemon-peel mixed with the above is an improvement, and a great authority in culinary matters suggests the addition of a little cayenne pepper in gingerbread. Whether it be advisable to use the latter ingredient or not, we leave our readers to decide. *Time.*—20 minutes to ½ hour. *Average cost,* 1*s.* to 1*s.* 4*d.* per lb. *Seasonable* at any time.

## GLAZE for covering Cold Hams, Tongues, &c.

*Ingredients.*—Stock, doubling the quantity of meat in the recipes. *Mode.*—We may remark at the outset, that unless glaze is wanted in very large quantities, it is seldom made expressly. Either of the stocks, boiled down and reduced very considerably, will be found to produce a very good glaze. Put the stock into a stewpan, over a nice clear fire; let it boil till it becomes somewhat stiff, when keep stirring, to prevent its burning. The moment it is sufficiently reduced, and come to a glaze, turn it into the glaze-pot before it gets cold. As, however, this is not to be found in every establishment, a white earthenware jar would answer the purpose; and this may be placed in a vessel of boiling water, to melt the glaze when required. It should never be warmed in a saucepan, except on the principle of the bain marie, lest it should reduce too much, and become black and bitter. If the glaze is wanted of a pale colour, more veal than beef should be used in making the stock; and it is as well to omit turnips and celery, as those impart a disagreeable bitter flavour.

**GLAZE-KETTLE.**

**GLAZE-KETTLE.**

This is a kettle used for keeping the strong stock boiled down to a jelly, which is known by the name of glaze. It is composed of two tin vessels, as shown in the cut, one of which, the upper,—containing the glaze, is inserted into one of larger diameter, and containing boiling water.

## GLAZE, to, Cold Joints, &c.

Melt the glaze by placing the vessel which contains it, into the bain marie or saucepan of boiling water; brush it over the meat with a paste-brush, and if in places it is not quite covered, repeat the operation. The glaze should not be too dark a colour.

## GOLDEN PUDDING.

*Ingredients.*—¼ lb. of bread-crumbs, ¼ lb. of suet, ¼ lb. of marmalade, ¼ lb. of sugar, 4 eggs. *Mode.*—Put the bread-crumbs into a basin; mix with them the suet, which should be finely minced, the marmalade, and the sugar; stir all these ingredients well together, beat the eggs to a froth, moisten the pudding with these, and when well mixed put it into a mould or buttered basin; tie down with a floured cloth, and boil for 2 hours. When turned out, strew a little fine-sifted sugar over the top, and serve. *Time.*—2 hours. *Average cost,* 11d. *Sufficient* for 5 or 6 persons. *Seasonable* at any time.

*Note.*—The mould may be ornamented with stoned raisins, arranged in any fanciful pattern, before the mixture is poured in, which would add very much to the appearance of the pudding. For a plainer pudding, double the quantities of the bread-crumbs; and if the eggs do not moisten it sufficiently, use a little milk.

## GOOSE, Green.

*Ingredients.*—Goose, 3 oz. of butter, pepper and salt to taste. *Mode.*—Geese are called green till they are about four months old, and should not be stuffed. After it has been singed and trussed, put into the body a seasoning of pepper and salt, and the butter to moisten it inside. Roast before a clear fire for about ¾ hour, froth and brown it nicely, and serve with a brown gravy, and, when liked, gooseberry-sauce. This dish should be garnished with water-cresses. *Time.*—About ¾ hour. *Average cost*, 4s. 6d. each. *Sufficient* for 5 or 6 persons. *Seasonable* in June, July, and August.

## GOOSE, Hashed.

[COLD MEAT COOKERY.] *Ingredients.*—The remains of cold roast goose, 2 onions, 2 oz. of butter, 1 pint of boiling water, 1 dessertspoonful of flour, pepper and salt to taste, 1 tablespoonful of port wine, 2 tablespoonfuls of mushroom ketchup. *Mode.*—Cut up the goose into pieces of the size required; the inferior joints, trimmings, &c., put into a stewpan to make the gravy; slice and fry the onions in the butter of a very pale brown; add these to the trimmings, and pour over about a pint of boiling water; stew these gently for ¾ hour, then skim and strain the liquor. Thicken it with flour, and flavour with port wine and ketchup in the above proportion; add a seasoning of pepper and salt, and put in the pieces of goose; let these get thoroughly hot through, but do not allow them to boil, and serve with sippets of toasted bread. *Time.*—Altogether, rather more than 1 hour. *Average cost*, exclusive of the cold goose, 4d. *Seasonable* from September to March.

## GOOSE, Roast.

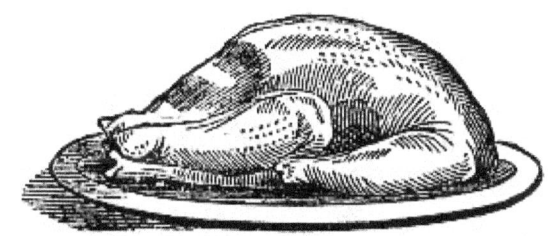

# ROAST GOOSE.

*Ingredients.*—Goose, 4 large onions, 10 sage-leaves, ¼ lb. of bread-crumbs, 1½ oz. of butter, salt and pepper to taste, 1 egg. *Choosing and Trussing.*—Select a goose with a clean white skin, plump breast, and yellow feet: if these latter are red, the bird is old. Should the weather permit, let it hang for a few days; by so doing the flavour will be very much improved. Pluck, singe, draw, and carefully wash and wipe the goose; cut off the neck close to the back, leaving the skin long enough to turn over; cut off the feet at the first joint, and separate the pinions at the first joint. Beat the breastbone flat with a rolling-pin, put a skewer through the under part of each wing, and having drawn up the legs closely, put a skewer into the middle of each, and pass the same quite through the body. Insert another skewer into the small of the leg, bring it close down to the side-bone, run it through, and do the same to the other side. Now cut off the end of the vent, and make a hole in the skin sufficiently large for the passage of the rump, in order to keep in the seasoning. *Mode.*—Make a sage-and-onion stuffing of the above ingredients, put it into the body of the goose, and secure it firmly at both ends by passing the rump through the hole made in the skin, and the other end by tying the skin of the neck to the back: by this means the seasoning will not escape. Put it down to a brisk fire, keep it well basted, and roast from 1½ to 2 hours, according to the size. Remove the skewers, and serve with a tureen of good gravy, and one of well-made apple sauce. Should a very highly-flavoured seasoning be preferred, the onions should not be parboiled, but minced raw: of the two methods the mild seasoning is far superior. A ragoût, or pie, should be made of the giblets, or they may be stewed down to make gravy. Be careful to serve the goose before the breast falls, or its appearance will be spoiled by coming flattened to table. As this is rather a troublesome joint to carve, a *large* quantity of gravy should not be poured round the goose, but sent in a tureen. *Time.*—A large goose, 1¾ hour; a moderate-sized one, 1/¼ to 1½ hour. *Seasonable* from September to March; but in perfection from Michaelmas to Christmas. *Average cost*, 5*s.* 6*d.* each. *Sufficient* for 8 or 9 persons.

*Note.*—A teaspoonful of made mustard, a saltspoonful of salt, a few grains of cayenne, mixed with a glass of port wine, are sometimes poured into the goose by a slit made in the apron. This sauce is by many considered an improvement.

# GOOSE, Roast, to Carve.

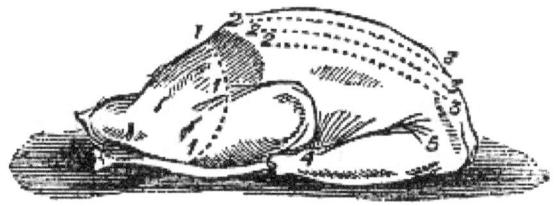

**ROAST GOOSE.**

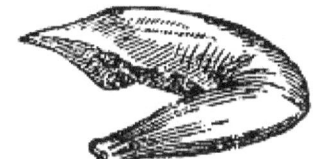

**LEG, WING, AND NECK-BONE OF GOOSE.**

It would not be fair to say that this dish bodes a great deal of happiness to an inexperienced carver, especially if there is a large party to serve, and the slices off the breast should not suffice to satisfy the desires and cravings of many wholesome appetites, produced, may be, by the various sports in vogue at Michaelmas and Christmas. The beginning of the task, however, is not in any way difficult. Evenly-cut slices, not too thick or too thin, should be carved from the breast in the direction of the line from 2 to 3; after the first slice has been cut, a hole should be made with the knife in the part called the apron, passing it round the line as indicated by the figures 1, 1, 1; here the stuffing is located, and some of this should be served on each plate, unless it is discovered that it is not agreeable to the taste of some one guest. If the carver manages cleverly, he will be able to cut a very large number of fine slices off the breast, and the more so if he commences close down by the wing, and carves upwards towards the ridge of the breastbone. As many slices as can be taken from the breast being carved, the wings should be cut off, and the same process as described in carving boiled fowl is made use of in this instance, only more dexterity and greater force will most probably be required. The shape of the leg, when disengaged from the body of the goose, should be like that shown in the accompanying engraving. It will be necessary, perhaps, in taking off the leg, to turn the goose on its side, and then, pressing down the small end of the leg, the knife should be passed under it from the top quite down to the joint; the leg being now turned back by the fork, the knife must cut through the joint, loosening the thighbone from its socket. The merrythought, which in a goose is not so large as might be expected, is disengaged in the same way as that of a fowl—by passing the knife under it, and pressing it backwards towards the neck. The neckbones, of which we give a cut, are freed by the same process as are those of a fowl; and the same may be said of all the other parts of this bird. The breast of a goose is the part most esteemed; all parts, however, are good, and full of juicy flavour.

### GOOSE STUFFING, Soyer's Recipe for.

Take 4 apples peeled and cored, 4 onions, 4 leaves of sage, and 4 leaves of lemon thyme not broken, and boil them in a stewpan with sufficient water to cover them; when done, pulp them through a sieve, removing the sage and thyme; then add sufficient pulp of mealy potatoes to cause it to be sufficiently dry without sticking to the hand; add pepper and salt, and stuff the bird.

### GOOSEBERRIES, Compôte of.

*Ingredients.*—Syrup; to 1 pint of syrup allow nearly a quart of gooseberries. *Mode.*—Top and tail the gooseberries, which should not be very ripe, and pour over them some boiling water; then take them out and plunge them into cold water with which has been mixed a tablespoonful of vinegar, which will assist to keep the fruit a good colour. Make a pint of syrup, and when it boils drain the gooseberries and put them in; simmer them gently until the fruit is nicely pulped and tender without being broken; then dish the gooseberries on a glass dish, boil the syrup for 2 or 3 minutes, pour over the gooseberries, and serve cold. *Time.*—About 5 minutes to boil the gooseberries in the syrup, 3 minutes to reduce the syrup. *Average cost,*

9*d*. *Sufficient.*—A quart of gooseberries for 5 or 6 persons. *Seasonable* in June.

## GOOSEBERRY CHIPS. (Useful for Dessert.)

*Ingredients.*—Gooseberries unripe and green, but quite full-grown; sifted loaf sugar. *Mode.*—Put the gooseberries, when cleaned of tops and tails, into jars, and boil them in a copper till quite soft. To every lb. of pulp put ½ lb. of loaf sugar sifted: the sugar must be stirred in very gently. Then pour out the sweetened pulp on flat dishes, about ⅛ inch thick, which must be set in the sun to dry. When sufficiently dried in the sun, the pulp may be cut into strips, and twisted into any fanciful shapes, bows, &c. *Time* for drying, according to the amount of sun. *Seasonable* at all times.

*Note.*—These chips may be kept for years in tin boxes, if packed quite dry, with layers of paper between the rows.

## GOOSEBERRY FOOL.

*Ingredients.*—Green gooseberries; to every pint of pulp add 1 pint of milk, or ½ pint of cream and ½ pint of milk; sugar to taste. *Mode.*—Cut the tops and tails off the gooseberries, put them into a jar with 2 tablespoonfuls of water and a little good moist sugar; set this jar in a saucepan of boiling water, and let it boil until the fruit is soft enough to mash. When done enough, beat it to a pulp, work this pulp through a colander, and stir to every pint the above proportion of milk, or equal quantities of milk and cream. Ascertain if the mixture is sweet enough, and put in plenty of sugar, or it will not be eatable; and in mixing the milk and gooseberries add the former very gradually to these: serve in a glass dish, or in small glasses. This, although a very old-fashioned and homely dish, is, when well made, very delicious, and, if properly sweetened, a very suitable preparation for children. *Time.*—From ¾ to 1 hour. *Average cost,* 6*d*. per pint, with milk. *Sufficient.*—A pint of milk and a pint of gooseberry pulp for 5 or 6 children. *Seasonable* in May and June.

## GOOSEBERRY JAM.

*Ingredients.*—To every lb. of fruit allow ¾ lb. of loaf sugar; currant-juice. *Mode.*—Select red hairy gooseberries; have them gathered in dry weather, when quite ripe, without being too soft. Weigh them; with a pair of scissors cut off the tops and tails, and to every 6 lbs. of fruit have ready ½ pint of red-currant juice, drawn as for jelly. Put the gooseberries and currant-juice into a preserving-pan, let them boil tolerably quickly, keeping them well stirred; when they begin to break, add to them the sugar, and keep simmering until the jam becomes firm, carefully skimming and stirring it, that it does not burn at the bottom. It should be boiled rather a long time, or it will not keep. Put it into pots (not too large), let it get perfectly cold, then cover the pots down with oiled and egged papers. *Time.*—About 1 hour to boil the gooseberries in the currant-juice, from ½ to ¾ hour with the sugar. *Average cost,* per lb. pot, from 6*d.* to 8*d.* *Sufficient.*—Allow 1½ pint of fruit for a lb. pot. *Seasonable.*—Make this in June or July.

## GOOSEBERRY JAM.

*Ingredients.*—To every 8 lbs. of red, rough, ripe gooseberries allow 1 quart of red-currant juice, 5 lbs. of loaf sugar. *Mode.*—Have the fruit gathered in dry weather, and cut off the tops and tails. Prepare 1 quart of red-currant juice, the same as for red-currant jelly; put it into a preserving-pan with the sugar, and keep stirring until the latter is dissolved. Keep it boiling for about 5 minutes; skim well; then put in the gooseberries, and let them boil from ½ to ¾ hour; then turn the whole into an earthen pan, and let it remain for 2 days. Boil the jam up again until it looks clear; put it into pots, and when cold, cover with oiled paper, and over the jars put tissue-paper brushed over on both sides with the white of an egg, and store away in a dry place. Care must be taken, in making this, to keep the jam well stirred and well skimmed, to prevent it burning at the bottom of the pan, and to have it very clear. *Time.*—5 minutes to boil the currant-juice and sugar after the latter is dissolved; from ½ to ¾ hour to simmer the gooseberries the first time, ¼ hour the second time of boiling. *Average cost,* from 8*d.* to 10*d.* per lb. pot. *Sufficient.*—Allow 1½ pint of fruit for a lb. pot. *Seasonable.*—Make this in June or July.

## GOOSEBERRY JAM, White or Green.

*Ingredients.*—Equal weight of fruit and sugar. *Mode.*—Select the gooseberries not very ripe, either white or green, and top and tail them. Boil the sugar with water (allowing ½ pint to every lb.) for about ¼ hour, carefully removing the scum as it rises; then put in the gooseberries, and simmer gently till clear and firm: try a little of the jam on a plate; if it jellies when cold, it is done, and should then be poured into pots. When cold, cover with oiled paper, and tissue-paper brushed over on both sides with the unbeaten white of an egg, and stow away in a dry place. *Time.*—¼ hour to boil the sugar and water, ¾ hour the jam. *Average cost*, from 6*d.* to 8*d.* per lb. pot. *Sufficient.*—Allow 1½ pint of fruit for a lb. pot. *Seasonable.*—Make this in June.

## GOOSEBERRY JELLY.

*Ingredients.*—Gooseberries; to every pint of juice allow ¾ lb. of loaf sugar. *Mode.*—Put the gooseberries, after cutting off the tops and tails, into a preserving-pan, and stir them over the fire until they are quite soft; then strain them through a sieve, and to every pint of juice allow ¾ lb. of sugar. Boil the juice and sugar together for nearly ¾ hour, stirring and skimming all the time; and if the jelly appears firm when a little of it is poured on to a plate, it is done, and should then be taken up and put into small pots. Cover the pots with oiled and egged papers, the same as for currant jelly, and store away in a dry place. *Time.*—¾ hour to simmer the gooseberries without the sugar; ¾ hour to boil the juice. *Average cost*, from 8*d.* to 10*d.* per ½-lb. pot. *Seasonable* in July.

## GOOSEBERRY PUDDING, Baked.

*Ingredients.*—Gooseberries, 3 eggs, 1½ oz. of butter, ½ pint of bread-crumbs, sugar to taste. *Mode.*—Put the gooseberries into a jar, previously cutting off the tops and tails; place this jar in boiling water, and let it boil until the gooseberries are soft enough to pulp; then beat them through a coarse sieve, and to every pint of pulp add 3 well-whisked eggs, 1½ oz. of butter, ½ pint of bread-crumbs, and sugar to taste; beat the mixture well, put a border of puff-paste round the edge of a pie-dish, put in the pudding, bake for about 40 minutes, strew sifted sugar over, and serve. *Time.*—About 40 minutes. *Average cost*, 10*d*. *Sufficient* for 4 or 5 persons. *Seasonable* from May to July.

## GOOSEBERRY PUDDING, Boiled.

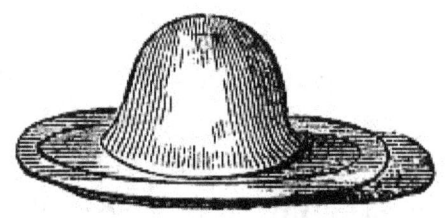

**BOILED FRUIT PUDDING**

*Ingredients.*—¾ lb. of suet crust, 1½ pint of green gooseberries, ¼ lb. of moist sugar. *Mode.*—Line a pudding-basin with suet crust rolled out to about ½ inch in thickness, and, with a pair of scissors, cut off the tops and tails of the gooseberries; fill the basin with the fruit, put in the sugar, and cover with crust. Pinch the edges of the pudding together, tie over it a floured cloth, put it into boiling water, and boil from 2½ to 3 hours; turn it out of the basin, and serve with a jug of cream. *Time.*—2½ to 3 hours. *Average cost*, 10*d*. *Sufficient* for 6 or 7 persons. *Seasonable* from May to July.

## GOOSEBERRY SAUCE for Boiled Mackerel.

*Ingredients.*—1 pint of green gooseberries, 3 tablespoonfuls of Béchamel (veal gravy may be substituted for this), 2 oz. of fresh butter; seasoning to taste of salt, pepper, and grated nutmeg. *Mode.*—Boil the gooseberries in water until quite tender; strain them, and rub them through a sieve. Put into a saucepan the Béchamel or gravy, with the butter and seasoning; add the pulp from the gooseberries, mix all well together, and heat gradually through. A little pounded sugar added to this sauce is by many persons considered an improvement, as the saccharine matter takes off the extreme acidity of the unripe fruit. *Time.*—Boil the gooseberries from 20 minutes to ½ hour. *Sufficient.*—This quantity, for a large dish of mackerel. *Seasonable* from May to July.

## GOOSEBERRY TART.

*Ingredients.*—1½ pint of gooseberries, ½ lb. of short crust, ¼ lb. of moist sugar. *Mode.*—With a pair of scissors cut off the tops and tails of the gooseberries; put them into a deep pie-dish, pile the fruit high in the centre, and put in the sugar; line the edge of the dish with short crust, put on the cover, and ornament the edges of the tart; bake in a good oven for about ¾ hour, and before being sent to table, strew over it some fine-sifted sugar. A jug of cream, or a dish of boiled or baked custards, should always accompany this dish. *Time.*—¾ hour. *Average cost*, 9*d*. *Sufficient* for 5 or 6 persons. *Seasonable* from May to July.

## GOOSEBERRY TRIFLE.

*Ingredients.*—1 quart of gooseberries, sugar to taste, 1 pint of custard, a plateful of whipped cream. *Mode.*—Put the gooseberries into a jar, with sufficient moist sugar to sweeten them, and boil them until reduced to a pulp. Put this pulp at the bottom of a trifle-dish; pour over it a pint of custard made by recipe, and, when cold, cover with whipped cream. The cream should be whipped the day before it is wanted for table, as it will then be so much firmer and more solid; but it should not be added to the fruit until a short time before it is required. The dish may be garnished as fancy dictates. *Time.*—About ¾ hour to boil the gooseberries. *Average cost*, 1*s*. 6*d*. *Sufficient* for 1 trifle. *Seasonable* in May, June, and July.

## GOOSEBERRY VINEGAR. (An Excellent Recipe.)

*Ingredients.*—2 pecks of crystal gooseberries, 6 gallons of water, 12 lbs. of foots sugar of the coarsest brown quality. *Mode.*—Mash the gooseberries (which should be quite ripe) in a tub with a mallet; put to them the water nearly milk-warm; let this stand 24 hours; then strain it through a sieve, and put the sugar to it; mix it well, and tun it. These proportions are for a 9-gallon cask; and if it be not quite full, more water must be added. Let the mixture be stirred from the bottom of the cask two or three times daily for three or four days, to assist the melting of the sugar; then paste a piece of linen cloth over the bunghole, and set the cask in a warm place, *but not in the sun*; any corner of a warm kitchen is the best situation for it. The following spring it should be drawn off into stone bottles, and the vinegar will be fit for use twelve months after it is made. This will be found a most excellent preparation, greatly superior to much that is sold under the name of the best white wine vinegar. Many years' experience has proved that pickle made with this vinegar will keep, when bought vinegar will not preserve the ingredients. The cost per gallon is merely nominal, especially to those who reside in the country and grow their own gooseberries; the coarse sugar is then the only ingredient to be purchased. *Time.*—To remain in the cask 9 months. *Average cost*, when the gooseberries have to be purchased, 1*s.* per gallon; when they are grown at home, 6*d.* per gallon. *Seasonable.*—This should be made the end of June or the beginning of July, when gooseberries are ripe and plentiful.

## GOOSEBERRY WINE, Effervescing.

*Ingredients.*—To every gallon of water allow 6 lbs. of green gooseberries, 3 lbs. of lump sugar. *Mode.*—This wine should be prepared from unripe gooseberries, in order to avoid the flavour which the fruit would give to the wine when in a mature state. Its briskness depends more upon the time of bottling than upon the unripe state of the fruit, for effervescing wine can be made from fruit that is ripe as well as that which is unripe. The fruit should be selected when it has nearly attained its full growth, and consequently before it shows any tendency to ripen. Any bruised or decayed berries, and those that are very small, should be rejected. The blossom and stalk ends should be removed, and the fruit well bruised in a tub or pan, in such quantities as to insure each berry being broken without crushing the seeds. Pour the water (which should be warm) on the fruit, squeeze and stir it with the hand until all the pulp is removed from the skin and seeds, and cover the whole closely for 24 hours; after which, strain it through a coarse bag, and press it with as much force as can be conveniently applied, to extract the whole of the juice and liquor the fruit may contain. To every 40 or 50 lbs. of fruit one gallon more of hot water may be passed through the *marc*, or husks, in order to obtain any soluble matter that may remain, and be again pressed. The juice should be put into a tub or pan of sufficient size to contain all of it, and the sugar added to it. Let it be well stirred until the sugar is dissolved, and place the pan in a warm situation; keep it closely covered, and let it ferment for a day or two. It must then be drawn off into clean casks, placed a little on one side for the scum that arises to be thrown out, and the casks kept filled with the remaining "must," that should be reserved for that purpose. When the active fermentation has ceased, the casks should be plugged upright, again filled, if necessary, the bungs be put in loosely, and, after a few days, when the fermentation is a little more languid (which may be known by the hissing noise ceasing), the bungs should be driven in tight, and a spile-hole made, to give vent if necessary. About November or December, on a clear fine day, the wine should be racked from its lees into clean casks, which may be rinsed with brandy. After a month, it should be examined to see if it is sufficiently clear for bottling; if not, it must be fined with isinglass, which may be dissolved in some of the wine: 1 oz. will be sufficient for 9 gallons. In bottling the wine, it will be necessary to wire the corks down, or to tie them down with string. Old champagne bottles are the best for this wine. In March or April, or when the gooseberry bushes begin to blossom, the wine must be bottled, in order to insure its being effervescing. *Seasonable.*— Make this the end of May or beginning of June, before the berries ripen.

## GRAVIES, General Stock for

By the addition of various store sauces, thickening and flavouring, good stock may be converted into good gravies. It should be borne in mind, however, that the goodness and strength of spices, wines, flavourings, &c., evaporate, and that they lose a great deal of their fragrance if added to the gravy a long time before they are wanted. If this point is attended to, a saving of one half the quantity of these ingredients will be effected, as, with long boiling, the flavour almost entirely passes away. The shank-bones of mutton, previously well soaked, will be found a great assistance in enriching gravies; a kidney or melt, beef skirt, trimmings of meat, &c. &c., answer very well when only a small quantity is wanted, and a good gravy need not necessarily be so very expensive; for economically-prepared dishes are oftentimes found as savoury and wholesome as dearer ones. The cook should also remember that the fragrance of gravies should not be overpowered by too much spice, or any strong essences, and that they should always be warmed in a *bain marie*, after they are flavoured, or else in a jar or jug placed in a saucepan full of boiling water. The remains of roast-meat gravy should always be saved; as, when no meat is at hand, a very nice gravy in haste may be made from it, and when added to hashes, ragoûts, &c., is a great improvement.

## GRAVY, a Good Beef, for Poultry, Game, &c.

*Ingredients.*—½ lb. of lean beef, ½ pint of cold water, 1 shalot or small onion, ½ a teaspoonful of salt, a little pepper, 1 tablespoonful of Harvey's sauce or mushroom ketchup, ½ a teaspoonful of arrowroot. *Mode.*—Cut up the beef into small pieces, and put it, with the water, into a stewpan. Add the shalot and seasoning, and simmer gently for 3 hours, taking care that it does not boil fast. A short time before it is required, take the arrowroot, and having mixed it with a little cold water, pour it into the gravy, which keep stirring, adding the Harvey's sauce, and just letting it boil. Strain off the gravy in a tureen, and serve very hot. *Time.*—3 hours. *Average cost*, 8d. per pint.

## GRAVY, Beef, a Quickly Made.

*Ingredients.*—½ lb. of shin of beef, ½ onion, ¼ carrot, 2 or 3 sprigs of parsley and savoury herbs, a piece of butter about the size of a walnut; cayenne and mace to taste, ¾ pint of water. *Mode.*—Cut up the meat into very small pieces, slice the onion and carrot, and put them into a small saucepan with the butter. Keep stirring over a sharp fire until they have taken a little colour, when add the water and the remaining ingredients. Simmer for ½ hour, skim well, strain, and flavour, when it will be ready for use. *Time.*—½ hour. *Average cost*, for this quantity, 5d.

## GRAVY, Brown.

*Ingredients.*—2 oz. of butter, 2 large onions, 2 lbs. of shin of beef, 2 small slices of lean bacon (if at hand), salt and whole pepper to taste, 3 cloves, 2 quarts of water. For thickening, 2 oz. of butter, 3 oz. of flour. *Mode.*—Put the butter into a stewpan; set this on the fire, throw in the onions cut in rings, and fry them a light brown; then add the beef and bacon, which should be cut into small square pieces; season, and pour in a teacupful of water; let it boil for about ten minutes, or until it is of a nice brown colour, occasionally stirring the contents. Now fill up with water in the above proportion; let it boil up, when draw it to the side of the fire to simmer very gently for 1½ hour; strain, and when cold, take off all the fat. In thickening this gravy, melt 3 oz. of butter in a stewpan, add 2 oz. of flour, and stir till of a light-brown colour; when cold, add it to the strained gravy, and boil it up quickly. This thickening may be made in larger quantities, and kept in a stone jar for use when wanted. *Time.*—Altogether, 2 hours. *Average cost*, 4*d.* per pint.

## GRAVY, Brown, without Meat.

*Ingredients.*—2 large onions, 1 large carrot, 2 oz. of butter, 3 pints of boiling water, 1 bunch of savoury herbs, a wineglassful of good beer; salt and pepper to taste. *Mode.*—Slice, flour, and fry the onions and carrots in the butter until of a nice light-brown colour, then add the boiling water and the remaining ingredients; let the whole stew gently for about an hour, then strain, and when cold, skim off all the fat. Thicken it, and, if thought necessary, add a few drops of colouring. *Time.*—1 hour. *Average cost*, 2*d.* per pint.

*Note.*—The addition of a small quantity of mushroom ketchup or Harvey's sauce very much improves the flavour of this gravy.

## GRAVY, Cheap, for Minced Veal

*Ingredients.*—Bones and trimmings of cold roast or boiled veal, 1½ pint of water, 1 onion, ¼ teaspoonful of minced lemon-peel, ¼ teaspoonful of salt, 1 blade of pounded mace, the juice of ¼ lemon; thickening of butter and flour. *Mode.*—Put all the ingredients into a stewpan, except the thickening and lemon-juice, and let them simmer very gently for rather more than 1 hour, or until the liquor is reduced to a pint, when strain through a hair sieve. Add a thickening of butter and flour, and the lemon-juice; set it on the fire, and let it just boil up, when it will be ready for use. It may be flavoured with a little tomato sauce, and, where a rather dark-coloured gravy is not objected to, ketchup, or Harvey's sauce, may be added at pleasure. *Time.*—Rather more than 1 hour. *Average cost*, 3*d.*

## GRAVY, Cheap, for Hashes, &c.

*Ingredients.*—Bones and trimmings of the cooked joint intended for hashing, ¼ teaspoonful of salt, ¼ teaspoonful of whole pepper, ¼ teaspoonful of whole allspice, a small faggot of savoury herbs, ½ head of celery, 1 onion, 1 oz. of butter, thickening, sufficient boiling water to cover the bones. *Mode.*—Chop the bones in small pieces, and put them in a stewpan, with the trimmings, salt, pepper, spice, herbs, and celery. Cover with boiling water, and let the whole simmer gently for 1½ or 2 hours. Slice and fry the onion in the butter till it is of a pale brown, and mix it gradually with the gravy made from the bones; boil for ¼ hour, and strain into a basin; now put it back into the stewpan; flavour with walnut pickle or ketchup, pickled-onion liquor, or any store sauce that may be preferred. Thicken with a little butter and flour, kneaded together on a plate, and the gravy will be ready for use. After the thickening is added, the gravy should just boil, to take off the rawness of the flour. *Time.*—2 hours, or rather more. *Average cost*, 4d., exclusive of the bones and trimmings.

## GRAVY for Roast Meat.

*Ingredients.*—Gravy, salt. *Mode.*—Put a common dish with a small quantity of salt in it under the meat, about a quarter of an hour before it is removed from the fire. When the dish is full, take it away, baste the meat, and pour the gravy into the dish on which the joint is to be served.

## GRAVY for Venison.

*Ingredients.*—Trimmings of venison, 3 or 4 mutton shank-bones, salt to taste, 1 pint of water, 2 teaspoonfuls of walnut ketchup. *Mode.*—Brown the trimmings over a nice clear fire, and put them in a stewpan with the shank-bones and water; simmer gently for 2 hours, strain and skim, and add the walnut ketchup and a seasoning of salt. Let it just boil, when it is ready to serve. *Time.*—2 hours.

## GRAVY, Jugged (Excellent).

*Ingredients.*—2 lbs. of shin of beef, ¼ lb. of lean ham, 1 onion or a few shalots, 2 pints of water, salt and whole pepper to taste, 1 blade of mace, a faggot of savoury herbs, ½ a large carrot, ½ a head of celery. *Mode.*—Cut up the beef and ham into small pieces, and slice the vegetables; take a jar, capable of holding two pints of water, and arrange therein, in layers, the ham, meat, vegetables, and seasoning, alternately, filling up with the above quantity of water; tie down the jar, or put a plate over the top, so that the steam may not escape; place it in the oven, and let it remain there from 6 to

8 hours; should, however, the oven be very hot, less time will be required. When sufficiently cooked, strain the gravy, and when cold, remove the fat. It may be flavoured with ketchup, wines, or any other store sauce that may be preferred. It is a good plan to put the jar in a cool oven over-night, to draw the gravy; and then it will not require so long baking the following day. *Time.*—From 6 to 8 hours, according to the oven. *Average cost*, 7*d.* per pint.

## GRAVY-KETTLE.

This is a utensil which will not be found in every kitchen; but it is a useful one where it is necessary to keep gravies hot for the purpose of pouring over various dishes as they are cooking. It is made of copper, and should, consequently, be heated over the hot-plate, if there be one, or a charcoal stove.

**GRAVY-KETTLE.**

## GRAVY made without Meat for Fowls.

*Ingredients.*—The necks, feet, livers, and gizzards of the fowls, 1 slice of toasted bread, ½ onion, 1 faggot of savoury herbs, salt and pepper to taste, ½ pint of water, thickening of butter and flour, 1 dessertspoonful of ketchup. *Mode.*—Wash the feet of the fowls thoroughly clean, and cut them and the neck into small pieces. Put these into a stewpan with the bread, onion, herbs, seasoning, livers, and gizzards; pour the water over them and simmer gently for 1 hour. Now take out the liver, pound it, and strain the liquor to it. Add a thickening of butter and flour, and a flavouring of mushroom ketchup; boil it up and serve. *Time.*—1 hour. *Average cost*, 4*d.* per pint.

## GRAVY, Rich, for Hashes, Ragoûts, &c.

*Ingredients.*—2 lbs. of shin of beef, l large onion or a few shalots, a little flour, a bunch of savoury herbs, 2 blades of mace, 2 or 3 cloves, 4 whole allspice, ¼ teaspoonful of whole pepper, 1 slice of lean ham or bacon, ½ a head of celery (when at hand), 2 pints of boiling water; salt and cayenne to taste. *Mode.*—Cut, the beef into thin slices, as also the onions, dredge them with flour, and fry of a pale brown, but do not allow them to get black; pour in the boiling water, let it boil up, and skim. Add the remaining ingredients, and simmer the whole very gently for 2 hours, or until all the juices are extracted from the meat; put it by to get cold, when take off all the fat. This gravy may be flavoured with ketchup, store sauces, wine, or, in fact, anything that may give additional and suitable relish to the dish it is intended for. *Time.*—Rather more than 2 hours. *Average cost,* 8*d.* per pint.

## GRAVY SOUP.

*Ingredients.*—6 lbs. of shin of beef, a knuckle of veal weighing 5 lbs., a few pieces or trimmings, 2 slices of nicely-flavoured lean ham; ¼ lb. of butter, 4 onions, 4 carrots, 1 turnip, nearly a head of celery, 3 blades of mace, 6 cloves, a bunch of savoury herbs, seasoning of salt and pepper to taste, 3 lumps of sugar, 6 quarts of boiling soft water. It can be flavoured with ketchup, Leamington sauce, Harvey's sauce, and a little soy. *Mode.*—Slightly brown the meat and ham in the butter, but do not let them burn. When this is done, pour to it the water, and as the scum rises, take it off; when no more appears, add all the other ingredients, and let the soup simmer slowly by the fire for 6 hours without stirring it any more from the bottom; take it off, and let it settle; skim off all the fat you can, and pass it through a sieve or cloth. When perfectly cold you can remove all the fat, and leave the sediment untouched, which serves very nicely for thick gravies, hashes, &c. *Time.*—7 hours. *Average cost,* 1*s.* per quart. *Seasonable* all the year. *Sufficient* for 14 persons.

## GRAVY, Veal, for White Sauces, Fricassees, &c.

*Ingredients.*—2 slices of nicely-flavoured lean ham, any poultry trimmings, 3 lbs. of lean veal, a faggot of savoury herbs, including parsley, a few green onions (or 1 large onion may be substituted for these), a few mushrooms, when obtainable; 1 blade of mace, salt to taste, 3 pints of water. *Mode.*—Cut up the ham and veal into small square pieces, put these in a stewpan, moistening them with a small quantity of water; place them over the fire to draw down. When the bottom of the stewpan becomes covered with a white glaze, fill up with water in the above proportion; add the remaining ingredients, stew very slowly for 3 or 4 hours, and do not forget to skim well the moment it boils. Put it by, and when cold take off all the fat. This may be used for Béchamel, sauce tournée, and many other white sauces. *Time.*—3 or 4 hours. *Average cost*, 9*d*. per pint.

## GREENGAGE JAM.

*Ingredients.*—To every lb. of fruit, weighed before being stoned, allow ¾ lb. of lump sugar. *Mode.*—Divide the greengages, take out the stones, and put them into a preserving-pan. Bring the fruit to a boil, then add the sugar, and keep stirring it over a gentle fire until it is melted. Remove all the scum as it rises, and, just before the jam is done, boil it rapidly for 5 minutes. To ascertain when it is sufficiently boiled, pour a little on a plate, and if the syrup thickens and appears firm, it is done. Have ready half the kernels blanched; put them into the jam, give them one boil, and pour the preserve into pots. When cold, cover down with oiled papers, and, over these, tissue paper brushed over on both sides with the white of an egg. *Time.*—¾ hour after the sugar is added. *Average cost*, from 6*d*. to 8*d*. per lb. pot. *Sufficient.*—Allow about 1½ pint of fruit for every lb. pot of jam. *Seasonable.*—Make this in August or September.

## GREENGAGES, Compôte of.

*Ingredients.*—1 pint of syrup, 1 quart of greengages. *Mode.*—Make a syrup, skim it well, and put in the greengages when the syrup is boiling, having previously removed the stalks and stones from the fruit. Boil gently for ¼ hour, or until the fruit is tender; but take care not to let it break, as the appearance of the dish would be spoiled were the fruit reduced to a pulp. Take the greengages carefully out, place them on a glass dish, boil the syrup for another 5 minutes, let it cool a little, pour over the fruit, and, when cold, it will be ready for use. *Time.*—¼ hour to simmer the fruit, 5 minutes the syrup. *Average cost*, in full season, 10*d*. *Sufficient* for 4 or 5 persons. *Seasonable* in July, August, and September.

## GREENGAGES, to Preserve and Dry.

*Ingredients.*—To every lb. of sugar allow 1 lb. of fruit, ¼ pint of water. *Mode.*—For this purpose, the fruit must be used before it is quite ripe, and part of the stalk must be left on. Weigh the fruit, rejecting all that is in the least degree blemished, and put it into a lined saucepan with the sugar and water, which should have been previously boiled together to a rich syrup. Boil the fruit in this for 10 minutes, remove it from the fire, and drain the greengages. The next day, boil up the syrup and put in the fruit again, and let it simmer for 3 minutes, and drain the syrup away. Continue this process for 5 or 6 days, and the last time place the greengages, when drained, on a hair sieve, and put them in an oven or warm spot to dry; keep them in a box, with paper between each layer, in a place free from damp. *Time.*—10 minutes the first time of boiling. *Seasonable.*—Make this in August or September.

## GREENGAGES, Preserved in Syrup.

*Ingredients.*—To every lb. of fruit allow 1 lb. of loaf sugar, ¼ pint of water. *Mode.*—Boil the sugar and water together for about 10 minutes; divide the greengages, take out the stones, put the fruit into the syrup, and let it simmer gently until nearly tender. Take it off the fire, put it into a large pan, and, the next day, boil it up again for about 10 minutes with the kernels from the stones, which should be blanched. Put the fruit carefully into jars, pour over it the syrup, and, when cold, cover down, so that the air is quite excluded. Let the syrup be well skimmed both the first and second day of boiling, otherwise it will not be clear. *Time.*—10 minutes to boil the syrup; ¼ hour to simmer the fruit the first day, 10 minutes the second day. *Average cost*, from 6*d.* to 8*d.* per lb. pot. *Sufficient.*—Allow about 1 pint of fruit to fill a 1-lb. pot. *Seasonable.*—Make this in August or September.

## GREENS, Boiled Turnip.

*Ingredients.*—To each ½ gallon of water allow 1 heaped tablespoonful of salt; turnip-greens. *Mode.*—Wash the greens well in two or three waters, and pick off all the decayed and dead leaves; tie them in small bunches, and put them into plenty of boiling water, salted in the above proportion. Keep them boiling quickly, with the lid of the saucepan uncovered, and when tender, pour them into a colander; let them drain, arrange them in a vegetable-dish, remove the string that the greens were tied with, and serve. *Time.*—15 to 20 minutes. *Average cost*, 4*d*. for a dish for 3 persons. *Seasonable* in March, April, and May.

## GROUSE PIE.

*Ingredients.*—Grouse; cayenne, salt, and pepper to taste; 1 lb. of rump-steak, ½ pint of well-seasoned broth, puff-paste. *Mode.*—Line the bottom of a pie-dish with the rump-steak cut into neat pieces, and, should the grouse be large, cut them into joints; but, if small, they may be laid in the pie whole; season highly with salt, cayenne, and black pepper; pour in the broth, and cover with a puff-paste; brush the crust over with the yolk of an egg, and bake from ¾ to 1 hour. If the grouse is cut into joints, the backbones and trimmings will make the gravy, by stewing them with an onion, a little sherry, a bunch of herbs, and a blade of mace: this should be poured in after the pie is baked. *Time.*—¾ to 1 hour. *Average cost*, exclusive of the grouse, which are seldom bought, 1*s*. 9*d*. *Seasonable* from the 12th of August to the beginning of December.

**ROAST GROUSE.**

## GROUSE, Roast.

*Ingredients.*—Grouse, butter, a thick slice of toasted bread. *Mode.*—Let the birds hang as long as possible; pluck and draw them; wipe, but do not wash them, inside and out, and truss them without the head, the same as for a roast fowl. Many persons still continue to truss them with the head under the wing, but the former is now considered the most approved method. Put them down to a sharp clear fire; keep them well basted the whole of the time they are cooking, and serve them on a buttered toast, soaked in the dripping-pan, with a little melted butter poured over them, or with bread-sauce and gravy. *Time.*—½ hour; if liked very thoroughly done, 35 minutes.

*Average cost*, 2*s.* to 2*s.* 6*d.* the brace; but seldom bought. *Sufficient.*—2 for a dish. *Seasonable* from the 12th of August to the beginning of December.

## GROUSE, to Carve.

Grouse may be carved in the way first described in carving partridge. The backbone of the grouse is highly esteemed by many, and this part of many game birds is considered the finest-flavoured.

**ROAST GROUSE.**

## GROUSE SALAD (Soyer's Recipe improved.)

*Ingredients.*—8 eggs, butter, fresh salad, 2 or 3 grouse; for the sauce, 1 tablespoonful of minced shalot, 2 tablespoonfuls of pounded sugar, the yolks of 2 eggs, 1 teaspoonful of minced parsley, ¼ oz. of salt, 12 tablespoonfuls of oil, 4 tablespoonfuls of Chili vinegar, 1 gill of cream, 2 tablespoonfuls of chopped tarragon and chervil. *Mode.*—Boil the eggs hard, shell them, throw them into cold water, cut a thin slice off the bottom to facilitate the proper placing of them in the dish, cut each one into four lengthwise, and make a very thin flat border of butter, about one inch from the edge of the dish the salad is to be served on; fix the pieces of egg upright close to each other, the yolk outside, or the yolk and white alternately; lay in the centre a fresh salad of whatever is in season, and, having previously roasted the grouse rather underdone, cut it into eight or ten pieces, and prepare the sauce as follows:—Put the shalots into a basin, with the sugar, the yolk of an egg, the parsley, and salt, and mix in by degrees the oil and vinegar; when all the ingredients are well mixed, put the sauce on ice or in a cool place. When ready to serve, whip the cream rather thick, which lightly mix with it; then lay the inferior parts of the grouse on the salad, sauce over so as to cover each piece, then lay over the salad and the remainder of the grouse, pour the rest of the sauce over, and serve. The eggs may be ornamented with a little dot of radishes or beetroot on the point. Anchovy and gherkin, cut into small diamonds, may be placed between, or cut gherkins in slices, and a border of them laid round. Tarragon or chervil-leaves are also a pretty addition. The remains of cold black-game, pheasant, or partridge may be used in the above manner, and will make a very delicate dish. *Average cost*, 2*s.* 6*d.* *Seasonable* from the 12th of August to the beginning of December.

## GRUEL, to make.

*Ingredients.*—1 tablespoonful of Robinson's patent groats, 2 tablespoonfuls of cold water, 1 pint of boiling water. *Mode.*—Mix the prepared groats smoothly with the cold water in a basin; pour over them the boiling water, stirring it all the time. Put it into a very clean saucepan; boil the gruel for 10 minutes, keeping it well stirred; sweeten to taste, and serve. It may be flavoured with a small piece of lemon-peel, by boiling it in the gruel, or a little grated nutmeg may be put in; but in these matters the taste of the patient should be consulted. Pour the gruel in a tumbler, and serve. When wine is allowed to the invalid, 2 tablespoonfuls of sherry or port make this preparation very nice. In cases of colds, the same quantity of spirits is sometimes added instead of wine. *Time.*—10 minutes. *Sufficient* to make a pint of gruel.

## GUDGEONS.

*Ingredients.*—Egg and bread-crumbs sufficient for the quantity of fish; hot lard. *Mode.*—Do not scrape off the scales, but take out the gills and inside, and cleanse thoroughly; wipe them dry, flour and dip them into egg, and sprinkle over with bread-crumbs. Fry of a nice brown. *Time.*—3 or 4 minutes. *Average cost.*—Seldom bought. *Seasonable* from March to July. *Sufficient.*—3 for each person.

## GUINEA-FOWL, Roast, Larded.

*Ingredients.*—A guinea-fowl, lardoons, flour, and salt. *Mode.*—When this bird is larded, it should be trussed the same as a pheasant; if plainly roasted, truss it like a turkey. After larding and trussing it, put it down to roast at a brisk fire; keep it well basted, and a short time before serving, dredge it with a little flour, and let it froth nicely. Serve with a little gravy in the dish, and a tureen of the same, and one of well-made bread-sauce. *Time.*—Guinea-fowl, larded, 1¼ hour; plainly roasted, about 1 hour. *Sufficient* for 6 persons. *Seasonable* in winter.

*Note.*—The breast, if larded, should be covered with a piece of paper, and removed about 10 minutes before serving.

## GURNET, or GURNARD.

*Ingredients.*—1 gurnet, 6 oz. of salt to each gallon of water. *Mode.*—Cleanse the fish thoroughly, and cut off the fins; have ready some boiling water, with salt in the above proportion; put the fish in, and simmer very gently for ½ hour. Parsley and butter, or anchovy sauce, should be served with it. *Time.*—¼ hour. *Average cost.*—Seldom bought. *Seasonable* from October to March, but in perfection in October. *Sufficient.*—A middling-sized one for two persons.

*Note.*—This fish is frequently stuffed with forcemeat, and baked.

## HADDOCK, Baked.

*Ingredients.*—A nice forcemeat, butter to taste, egg and bread-crumbs. *Mode.*—Scale and clean the fish, without cutting it open much; put in a nice delicate forcemeat, and sew up the slit. Brush it over with egg, sprinkle over bread-crumbs, and baste frequently with butter. Garnish with parsley and cut lemon, and serve with, a nice brown gravy, plain melted butter, or anchovy sauce. The egg and bread-crumbs can be omitted, and pieces of butter placed over the fish. *Time.*—Large haddock, ¾ hour; moderate size, ¼ hour. *Seasonable* from August to February. *Average cost*, from 9*d.* upwards.

*Note.*—Haddocks may be filleted, rubbed over with egg and bread-crumbs, and fried a nice brown; garnish with crisped parsley.

## HADDOCK, Boiled.

*Ingredients.*—Sufficient water to cover the fish; ¼ lb. of salt to each gallon of water. *Mode.*—Scrape the fish, take out the inside, wash it thoroughly, and lay it in a kettle, with enough water to cover it, and salt in the above proportion. Simmer gently from 15 to 20 minutes, or rather more, should the fish be very large. For small haddocks, fasten the tails in their mouths, and put them into boiling water. 10 to 15 minutes will cook them. Serve with plain melted butter, or anchovy sauce. *Time.*—Large haddock, ½ hour; small, ¼ hour, or rather less. *Average cost*, from 9*d.* upwards. *Seasonable* from August to February.

## HADDOCK, Dried.

Dried haddock should be gradually warmed through, either before or over a nice clear fire. Rub a little piece of butter over, just before sending it to table.

## HADDOCK, Dried.

*Ingredients.*—1 large thick haddock, 2 bay-leaves, 1 small bunch of savoury herbs, not forgetting parsley, a little butter and pepper; boiling water. *Mode.*—Cut up the haddock into square pieces, make a basin hot by means of hot water, which pour out. Lay in the fish, with the bay-leaves and herbs; cover with boiling water; put a plate over to keep in the steam, and let it remain for 10 minutes. Take out the slices, put them in a hot dish, rub over with butter and pepper, and serve. *Time.*—10 minutes. *Seasonable* at any time, but best in winter.

## HAM OMELET (a delicious Breakfast Dish).

*Ingredients.*—6 eggs, 4 oz. of butter, ½ saltspoonful of pepper, 2 tablespoonfuls of minced ham. *Mode.*—Mince the ham very finely, without any fat, and fry it for 2 minutes in a little butter; then make the batter for the omelet, stir in the ham, and proceed as in the case of a plain omelet. Do not add any salt to the batter, as the ham is usually sufficiently salt to impart a flavour to the omelet. Good lean bacon, or tongue, answers equally well for this dish; but they must also be slightly cooked previously to mixing them with the batter. Serve very hot and quickly, without gravy. *Time.*—From 4 to 6 minutes. *Average cost*, 1s. *Sufficient* for 4 persons. *Seasonable* at any time.

## HAM, FRIED, AND EGGS (a Breakfast Dish).

*Ingredients.*—Ham; eggs. *Mode.*—Cut the ham into slices, and take care that they are of the same thickness in every part. Cut off the rind, and if the ham should be particularly hard and salt, it will be found an improvement to soak it for about 10 minutes in hot water, and then dry it in a cloth. Put it into a cold frying-pan, set it over the fire, and turn the slices 3 or 4 times whilst they are cooking. When done, place them on a dish, which should be kept hot in front of the fire during the time the eggs are being poached. Poach the eggs, slip them on to the slices of ham, and serve quickly. *Time.*

—7 or 8 minutes to broil the ham. *Average cost*, 8*d*. to 1*s*. per lb. by the whole ham. *Sufficient.*—Allow 2 eggs and a slice of ham to each person. *Seasonable* at any time.

*Note.*—Ham may also be toasted or broiled; but, with the latter method, to insure its being well cooked, the fire must be beautifully clear, or it will have a smoky flavour far from agreeable.

## HAM, Potted, that will keep Good for some time.

*Ingredients.*—To 4 lbs. of lean ham allow 1 lb. of fat, 2 teaspoonfuls of pounded mace, ½ nutmeg grated, rather more than ½ teaspoonful of cayenne, clarified lard. *Mode.*—Mince the ham, fat and lean together in the above proportion, and pound it well in a mortar, seasoning it with cayenne pepper, pounded mace, and nutmeg; put the mixture into a deep baking-dish, and bake for ½ hour; then press it well into a stone jar, till up the jar with clarified lard, cover it closely, and paste over it a piece of thick paper. If well seasoned, it will keep a long time in winter, and will be found very convenient for sandwiches, &c. *Time.*—½ hour. *Seasonable* at any time.

## HAM, Potted (a nice addition to the Breakfast or Luncheon table).

*Ingredients.*—To 2 lbs. of lean ham allow ½ lb. of fat, 1 teaspoonful of pounded mace, ½ teaspoonful of pounded allspice, ½ nutmeg, pepper to taste, clarified butter. *Mode.*—Cut some slices from the remains of a cold ham, mince them small, and to every 2 lbs. of lean allow the above proportion of fat. Pound the ham in a mortar to a fine paste, with the fat, gradually add the seasonings and spices, and be very particular that all the ingredients are well mixed and the spices well pounded. Press the mixture into potting-pots, pour over clarified butter, and keep it in a cool place. *Average cost* for this quantity, 2*s*. 6*d*. *Seasonable* at any time.

## HAM, to Bake.

*Ingredients.*—Ham; a common crust. *Mode.*—As a ham for baking should be well soaked, let it remain in water for at least 12 hours. Wipe it dry, trim away any rusty places underneath, and cover it with a common crust, taking care that this is of sufficient thickness all over to keep the gravy in. Place it in a moderately-heated oven, and bake for nearly 4 hours. Take off the crust and skin, and cover with raspings, the same as for boiled ham, and garnish the knuckle with a paper frill. This method of cooking a ham is, by many persons, considered far superior to boiling it, as it cuts fuller of gravy and has a finer flavour, besides keeping a much longer time good. *Time.*—A medium-sized ham, 4 hours. *Average cost*, from 8*d.* to 1*s.* per lb. by the whole ham. *Seasonable* all the year.

## HAM, to Boil.

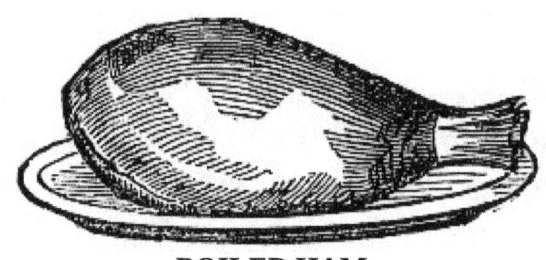

**BOILED HAM.**

*Ingredients.*—Ham, water, glaze, or raspings. *Mode.*—In choosing a ham, ascertain that it is perfectly sweet, by running a sharp knife into it, close to the bone; and if, when the knife is withdrawn, it has an agreeable smell, the ham is good; if, on the contrary, the blade has a greasy appearance and offensive smell, the ham is bad. If it has been long hung, and is very dry and salt, let it remain in soak for 24 hours, changing the water frequently. This length of time is only necessary in the case of its being very hard; from 8 to 12 hours would be sufficient for a Yorkshire or Westmoreland ham. Wash it thoroughly clean, and trim away from the under-side all the rusty and smoked parts, which would spoil the appearance. Put it into a boiling-pot, with sufficient cold water to cover it; bring it gradually to boil, and as the scum rises, carefully remove it. Keep it simmering very gently until tender, and be careful that it does not stop boiling, nor boil too quickly. When done, take it out of the pot, strip off the skin, and sprinkle over it a few fine bread-raspings, put a frill of cut paper round the knuckle, and serve. If to be eaten cold, let the ham remain in the water until nearly cold: by this method the juices are kept in, and it will be found infinitely superior to one taken out of the water hot; it should, however, be borne in mind that the ham must *not* remain in the saucepan *all* night. When the skin is removed, sprinkle over bread-raspings, or, if wanted particularly nice, glaze it. Place a paper frill round the knuckle, and garnish with parsley or cut vegetable flowers. *Time.*—A ham weighing 10 lbs., 4 hours to *simmer gently*; 15 lbs., 5 hours; a very large one, about 6 hours. *Average cost,* from 8*d.* to 1*s.* per lb. by the whole ham. *Seasonable* all the year.

## HAM, how to Boil to give it an excellent flavour.

*Ingredients.*—Vinegar and water, 2 heads of celery, 2 turnips, 3 onions, a large bunch of savoury herbs. *Mode.*—Prepare the ham as in the preceding recipe, and let it soak for a few hours in vinegar and water. Put it on in cold water, and when it boils, add the vegetables and herbs. Simmer very gently until tender, take it out, strip off the skin, cover with bread-raspings, and put a paper ruche or frill round the knuckle. *Time.*—A ham weighing 10 lbs., 4 hours. *Average cost,* 8*d.* to 1*s.* per lb. by the whole ham. *Seasonable* at any time.

## HAM, to Carve.

In cutting a ham, the carver must be guided according as he desires to practise economy, or have, at once, fine slices out of the prime part. Under the first supposition, he will commence at the knuckle end, and cut off thin slices towards the thick part of the ham. To reach the choicer portion, the knife, which must be very sharp and thin, should be carried quite down to the bone, in the direction of the line 1 to 2. The slices should be thin and even, and always cut down to the bone. There are some who like to carve a ham by cutting a hole at the top, and then slicing pieces off inside the hole, gradually enlarging the circle; but we think this is a plan not to be recommended. A ham, when hot, is usually sent to table with a paper ruffle round the knuckle.

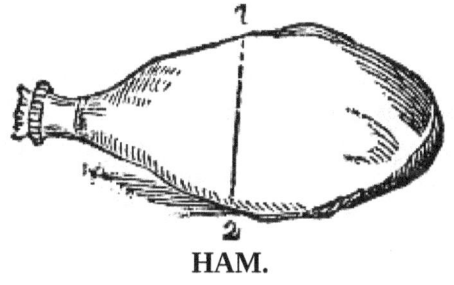

**HAM.**

## HAMS, for Curing (Mons. Ude's Recipe).

*Ingredients.*—For 2 hams weighing about 16 or 18 lbs. each, allow 1 lb. of moist sugar, 1 lb. of common salt, 2 oz. of saltpetre, 1 quart of good vinegar. *Mode.*—As soon as the pig is cold enough to be cut up, take the 2 hams and rub them well with common salt, and leave them in a large pan for 3 days. When the salt has drawn out all the blood, drain the hams, and throw the brine away. Mix sugar, salt, and saltpetre together in the above proportion, rub the hams well with these, and put them into a vessel large enough to hold them, always keeping the salt over them. Let them remain for 3 days, then pour over them a quart of good vinegar. Turn them in the brine every day for a month, then drain them well, and rub them with bran. Have them smoked over a wood fire, and be particular that the hams are hung as high up as possible from the fire; otherwise the fat will melt, and they will become dry and hard. *Time.*—To be pickled 1 month; to be smoked 1 month. *Sufficient* for 2 hams of 18 lbs. each. *Seasonable* from October to March.

## HAMS, to Cure Sweet, in the Westmoreland way.

*Ingredients.*—3 lbs. of common salt, 3 lbs. of coarse sugar, 1 lb. of bay-salt, 3 quarts of strong beer. *Mode.*—Before the hams are put into pickle, rub them the preceding day well with salt, and drain the brine well from them. Put the above ingredients into a saucepan, and boil for ¼ hour; pour over the hams, and let them remain a month in the pickle. Rub and turn them every day, but do not take them out of the pickling-pan; and have them smoked for a month. *Time.*—To be pickled 1 month; to be smoked 1 month. *Seasonable* from October to March.

## HAMS, to Pickle (Suffolk Recipe).

*Ingredients.*—To a ham from 10 to 12 lbs., allow 1 lb. of coarse sugar, ¾ lb. of salt, 1 oz. of saltpetre, ½ a teacupful of vinegar. *Mode.*—Rub the hams well with common salt, and leave them for a day or two to drain; then rub well in the above proportion of sugar, salt, saltpetre, and vinegar, and turn them every other day. Keep them in the pickle 1 month, drain them, and send them to be smoked over a wood fire for 3 weeks or a month. *Time.*—To remain in the pickle 1 month; to be smoked 3 weeks or 1 month.

*Sufficient.*—The above proportion of pickle is sufficient for 1 ham. *Seasonable.*—Hams should be pickled from October to March.

## HAMS, to Salt Two, about 12 or 15 lbs. each.

*Ingredients.*—2 lbs. of treacle, ½ lb. of saltpetre, 1 lb. of bay-salt, 2 pounds of common salt. *Mode.*—Two days before they are put into pickle, rub the hams well with salt, to draw away all slime and blood. Throw what comes from them away, and then rub them with treacle, saltpetre, and salt. Lay them in a deep pan, and let them remain one day; boil the above proportion of treacle, saltpetre, bay-salt, and common salt for ¼ hour, and pour this pickle boiling hot over the hams: there should be sufficient of it to cover them. For a day or two rub them well with it; afterwards they will only require turning. They ought to remain in this pickle for 3 weeks or a month, and then be sent to be smoked, which will take nearly or quite a month to do. An ox-tongue pickled in this way is most excellent, to be eaten either green or smoked. *Time.*—To remain in the pickle 3 weeks or a month; to be smoked about a month. *Seasonable* from October to March.

## HAMS, to Smoke, at Home.

Take an old hogshead, stop up all the crevices, and fix a place to put a cross-stick near the bottom, to hang the articles to be smoked on. Next, in the side, cut a hole near the top, to introduce an iron pan filled with sawdust and small pieces of green wood. Having turned the tub upside down, hang the articles upon the cross-stick, introduce the iron pan in the opening, and place a piece of red-hot iron in the pan, cover it with sawdust, and all will be complete. Let a large ham remain 40 hours, and keep up a good smoke. Fish may be smoked in the same manner.

## HARE, Broiled (a Supper or Luncheon Dish).

*Ingredients.*—The legs and shoulders of a roast hare, cayenne and salt to taste, a little butter. *Mode.*—Cut the legs and shoulders from a roast hare, season them highly with salt and cayenne, and broil them over a very clear fire for 5 minutes. Dish them on a hot dish, rub over them a little cold butter, and send to table very quickly. *Time.*—5 minutes. *Seasonable* from September to the end of February.

## HARE, Hashed.

[Cold Meat Cookery.] *Ingredients.*—The remains of cold roast hare, 1 blade of pounded mace, 2 or 3 allspice, pepper and salt to taste, 1 onion, a bunch of savoury herbs, 3 tablespoonfuls of port wine, thickening of butter and flour, 2 tablespoonfuls of mushroom ketchup. *Mode.*—Cut the cold hare into neat slices, and put the head, bones, and trimmings into a stewpan, with ¾ pint of water; add the mace, allspice, seasoning, onion, and herbs, and stew for nearly an hour, and strain the gravy; thicken it with butter and flour, add the wine and ketchup, and lay in the pieces of hare, with any stuffing that may be left. Let the whole gradually heat by the side of the fire, and, when it has simmered for about 5 minutes, serve, and garnish the dish with sippets of toasted bread. Send red-currant jelly to table with it. *Time.*—Rather more than 1 hour. *Average cost*, exclusive of the cold hare, 6*d. Seasonable* from September to the end of February.

## HARE, Jugged (very good).

*Ingredients.*—1 hare, 1½ lb. of gravy beef, ½ lb. of butter, 1 onion, 1 lemon, 6 cloves; pepper, cayenne, and salt to taste; ½ pint of port wine. *Mode.*—Skin, paunch, and wash the hare, cut it into pieces, dredge them with flour, and fry in boiling butter. Have ready 1½ pint of gravy, made from the above proportion of beef, and thickened with a little flour. Put this into a jar; add the pieces of fried hare, an onion stuck with six cloves, a lemon peeled and cut in half, and a good seasoning of pepper, cayenne, and salt; cover the jar down tightly, put it up to the neck into a stewpan of boiling water, and let it stew until the hare is quite tender, taking care to keep the water boiling. When nearly done, pour in the wine, and add a few forcemeat balls: these must be fried or baked in the oven for a few minutes before they are put to the gravy. Serve with red-currant jelly. *Time.*—3½ to 4 hours. If the hare is very old, allow 4½ hours. *Average cost*, 7*s. Sufficient* for 7 or 8 persons. *Seasonable* from September to the end of February.

## HARE, Jugged (a Quicker and more Economical Way).

*Ingredients.*—1 hare, a bunch of sweet herbs, 2 onions, each stuck with 3 cloves, 6 whole allspice, ½ teaspoonful of black pepper, a strip of lemon-peel, thickening of butter and flour, 2 tablespoonfuls of mushroom ketchup,

¼ pint of port wine. *Mode.*—Wash the hare nicely, cut it up into joints (not too large), and flour and brown them as in the preceding recipe; then put them into a stewpan with the herbs, onions, cloves, allspice, pepper, and lemon-peel; cover with hot water, and when it boils, carefully remove all the scum, and let it simmer gently till tender, which will be in about 1¾ hour, or longer, should the hare be very old. Take out the pieces of hare, thicken the gravy with flour and butter, add the ketchup and port wine, let it boil for about 10 minutes, strain it through a sieve over the hare, and serve. A few fried forcemeat balls should be added at the moment of serving, or, instead of frying them, they may be stewed in the gravy, about 10 minutes before the hare is wanted for table. Do not omit to serve red-currant jelly with it. *Time.*—Altogether 2 hours. *Average cost*, 5*s*. 6*d*. *Sufficient* for 7 or 8 persons. *Seasonable* from September to the end of February.

*Note.*—Should there be any left, re-warm it the next day by putting the hare, &c., into a covered jar, and placing this jar in a saucepan of boiling water; this method prevents a great deal of waste.

## HARE, Potted (a Luncheon or Breakfast Dish).

*Ingredients.*—1 hare, a few slices of bacon, a large bunch of savoury herbs, 4 cloves, ½ teaspoonful of whole allspice, 2 carrots, 2 onions, salt and pepper to taste, 1 pint of water, 2 glasses of sherry. *Mode.*—Skin, empty, and wash the hare; cut it down the middle, and put it into a stewpan, with a few slices of bacon under and over it; add the remaining ingredients, and stew very gently until the hare is tender, and the flesh will separate easily from the bones. When done enough, take it up, remove the bones, and pound the meat, *with the bacon,* in a mortar, until reduced to a perfectly smooth paste. Should it not be sufficiently seasoned, add a little cayenne, salt, and pounded mace, but be careful that these are well mixed with the other ingredients. Press the meat into potting-pots, pour over clarified butter, and keep in a dry place. The liquor that the hare was stewed in, should be saved for hashes, soups, &c. &c. *Time.*—About 2½ hours to stew the hare. *Seasonable* from September to the end of February.

## HARE, Roast.

**ROAST HARE.**

*Ingredients.*—Hare, forcemeat, a little milk, butter. *Choosing and Trussing.*—Choose a young hare; which may be known by its smooth and sharp claws, and by the cleft in the lip not being much spread. To be eaten in perfection, it must hang for some time; and, if properly taken care of, it may be kept for several days. It is better to hang without being paunched; but should it be previously emptied, wipe the inside every day, and sprinkle over it a little pepper and ginger, to prevent the musty taste which long keeping in the damp occasions, and also which affects the stuffing. After it is skinned, wash it well, and soak for an hour in warm water to draw out the blood; if old, let it lie in vinegar for a short time, but wash it well afterwards in several waters. Make a forcemeat, wipe the hare dry, fill the belly with it, and sew it up. Bring the hind and fore legs close to the body towards the head, run a skewer through each, fix the head between the shoulders by means of another skewer, and be careful to leave the ears on. Put a string round the body from skewer to skewer, and tie it above the back. *Mode.*—The hare should be kept at a distance from the fire when it is first laid down, or the outside will become dry and hard before the inside is done. Baste it well with milk for a short time, and afterwards with butter; and particular attention must be paid to the basting, so as to preserve the meat on the back juicy and nutritive. When it is almost roasted enough, flour the hare, and baste well with butter. When nicely frothed, dish it, remove the skewers, and send it to table with a little gravy in the dish, and a tureen of the same. Red-currant jelly must also not be forgotten, as this is an indispensable accompaniment to roast hare. For economy, good beef dripping may be substituted for the milk and butter to baste with; but the basting, as we have before stated, must be continued without intermission. If the liver is good, it may be parboiled, minced, and mixed with the stuffing; but it should not be used unless quite fresh. *Time.*—A middling-sized hare, 1¼ hour; a large hare, 1½ to 2 hours. *Average cost*, from 4*s.* to 6*s. Sufficient* for 5 or 6 persons. *Seasonable* from September to the end of February.

## HARE, Roast, to Carve.

The "Grand Carver" of olden times, a functionary of no ordinary dignity, was pleased when he had a hare to manipulate, for his skill and grace had an opportunity of display. *Diners à la Russe* may possibly, erewhile, save modern gentlemen the necessity of learning the art which was in auld lang syne one of the necessary accomplishments of the youthful squire; but, until side-tables become universal, or till we see the office of "grand carver" once more instituted, it will be well for all to learn how to assist at the carving of this dish, which, if not the most elegant in appearance, is a very general favourite. The hare, having its head to the left, as shown in the woodcut, should be first served by cutting slices from each side of the backbone, in the direction of the lines from 3 to 4. After these prime parts are disposed of, the leg should next be disengaged by cutting round the line indicated by the figures 5 to 6. The shoulders will then be taken off by passing the knife round from 7 to 8. The back of the hare should now be divided by cutting quite through its spine, as shown by the line 1 to 2, taking care to feel with the point of the knife for a joint where the back may be readily penetrated. It is the usual plan not to serve any bone in helping hare; and thus the flesh should be sliced from the legs and placed alone on the plate. In large establishments, and where men-cooks are kept, it is often the case that the backbone of the hare, especially in old animals, is taken out, and then the process of carving is, of course, considerably facilitated. A great point to be remembered in connection with carving hare is, that plenty of gravy should accompany each helping, otherwise this dish, which is naturally dry, will lose half its flavour, and so become a failure. Stuffing is also served with it; and the ears, which should be nicely crisp, and the brains of the hare, are esteemed as delicacies by many connoisseurs.

**ROAST HARE.**

## HARE SOUP.

*Ingredients.*—A hare fresh-killed, 1 lb. of lean gravy-beef, a slice of ham, 1 carrot, 2 onions, a faggot of savoury herbs, ¼ oz. of whole black pepper, a little browned flour, ¼ pint of port wine, the crumb of two French rolls, salt and cayenne to taste, 3 quarts of water. *Mode.*—Skin and paunch the hare, saving the liver and as much blood as possible. Cut it in pieces, and put it in a stewpan with all the ingredients, and simmer gently for 6 hours. This soup should be made the day before it is wanted. Strain through a sieve, put the best parts of the hare in the soup, and serve.

## HARE SOUP.

Proceed as above; but, instead of putting the joints of the hare in the soup, pick the meat from the bones, pound it in a mortar, and add it, with the crumb of two French rolls, to the soup. Rub all through a sieve; heat slowly, but do not let it boil. Send it to table immediately. *Time.*—8 hours. *Average cost*, 1*s.* 9*d.* per quart. *Seasonable* from September to February. *Sufficient* for 10 persons.

## HERB POWDER, for Flavouring when Fresh Herbs are not obtainable.

*Ingredients.*—1 oz. of dried lemon-thyme, 1 oz. of dried winter savory, 1 oz. of dried sweet marjoram and basil, 2 oz. of dried parsley, 1 oz. of dried lemon-peel. *Mode.*—Prepare and dry the herbs, pick the leaves from the stalks, pound them, and sift them through a hair sieve; mix in the above proportions, and keep in glass bottles, carefully excluding the air. This we think a far better method of keeping herbs, as the flavour and fragrance do not evaporate so much as when they are merely put in paper bags. Preparing them in this way, you have them ready for use at a moment's notice. Mint, sage, parsley, &c., dried, pounded, and each put into separate bottles, will be found very useful in winter.

## HERBS, to Dry, for Winter Use.

On a very dry day, gather the herbs, just before they begin to flower. If this is done when the weather is damp, the herbs will not be so good a colour. (It is very necessary to be particular in little matters like this, for trifles constitute perfection, and herbs nicely dried will be found very acceptable when frost and snow are on the ground. It is hardly necessary, however, to state that the flavour and fragrance of fresh herbs are incomparably finer.) They should be perfectly freed from dirt and dust, and be divided into small bunches, with their roots cut off. Dry them quickly in a very hot oven, or before the fire, as by this means most of their flavour will be preserved, and be careful not to burn them; tie them up in paper bags, and keep in a dry place. This is a very general way of preserving dried herbs; but we would recommend the plan described in a former recipe. *Seasonable.*—From the month of July to the end of September is the proper time for storing herbs for winter use.

## HERRINGS, White, Baked.

*Ingredients.*—12 herrings, 4 bay-leaves, 12 cloves, 12 allspice, 2 small blades of mace, cayenne pepper and salt to taste, sufficient vinegar to fill up the dish. *Mode.*—Take herrings, cut off the heads, and gut them. Put them in a pie-dish, heads and tails alternately, and, between each layer, sprinkle over the above ingredients. Cover the fish with the vinegar, and bake for ½ hour, but do not use it till quite cold. The herrings may be cut down the front, the backbone taken out, and closed again. Sprats done in this way are very delicious. *Time.*—½ an hour. *Average cost*, 1*d.* each.

To Choose the Herring.—The more scales this fish has, the surer the sign of its freshness. It should also have a bright and silvery look; but if red about the head, it is a sign that it has been dead for some time.

## HERRINGS, Red or YARMOUTH BLOATERS.

The best way to cook these is to make incisions in the skin across the fish, because they do not then require to be so long on the fire, and will be far better than when cut open. The hard roe makes a nice relish by pounding it in a mortar, with a little anchovy, and spreading it on toast. If very dry, soak in warm water 1 hour before dressing.

## HIDDEN MOUNTAIN, The (a pretty Supper Dish).

*Ingredients.*—6 eggs, a few slices of citron, sugar to taste, ¼ pint of cream, a layer of any kind of jam. *Mode.*—Beat the whites and yolks of the eggs separately; then mix them and beat well again, adding a few thin slices of citron, the cream, and sufficient pounded sugar to sweeten it nicely. When the mixture is well beaten, put it into a buttered pan, and fry the same as a pancake; but it should be three times the thickness of an ordinary pancake. Cover it with jam, and garnish with slices of citron and holly-leaves. This dish is served cold. *Time.*—About 10 minutes to fry the mixture. *Average cost,* with the jam, 1*s.* 4*d. Sufficient* for 3 or 4 persons. *Seasonable* at any time.

## HODGE-PODGE.

*Ingredients.*—2 lbs. of shin of beef, 3 quarts of water, 1 pint of table-beer, 2 onions, 2 carrots, 2 turnips, 1 head of celery; pepper and salt to taste; thickening of butter and flour. *Mode.*—Put the meat, beer, and water in a stewpan; simmer for a few minutes, and skim carefully. Add the vegetables and seasoning; stew gently till the meat is tender. Thicken with the butter and flour, and serve with turnips and carrots, or spinach and celery. *Time.*—3 hours, or rather more. *Average cost,* 3*d.* per quart. *Seasonable* at any time. *Sufficient* for 12 persons.

## HODGE-PODGE.

[Cold Meat Cookery.] *Ingredients.*—About 1 lb. of underdone cold mutton, 2 lettuces, 1 pint of green peas, 5 or 6 green onions, 2 oz. of butter, pepper and salt to taste, ½ teacupful of water. *Mode.*—Mince the mutton, and cut up the lettuces and onions in slices. Put those in a stewpan, with all the ingredients except the peas, and let these simmer very gently for ¾ hour, keeping them well stirred. Boil the peas separately, mix these with the mutton, and serve very hot. *Time.*—¾ hour. *Sufficient* for 3 or 4 persons. *Seasonable* from the end of May to August.

## HOLLY-LEAVES, to Frost, for Garnishing and Decorating Dessert and Supper Dishes.

*Ingredients.*—Sprigs of holly, oiled butter, coarsely-powdered sugar. *Mode.*—Procure some nice sprigs of holly; pick the leaves from the stalks, and wipe them with a clean cloth free from all moisture; then place them on a dish near the fire, to get thoroughly dry, but not too near to shrivel the leaves; dip them into oiled butter, sprinkle over them some coarsely-powdered sugar, and dry them before the fire. They should be kept in a dry place, as the least damp would spoil their appearance. *Time.*—About 10 minutes to dry before the fire. *Seasonable.*—These may be made at any time; but are more suitable for winter garnishes, when fresh flowers are not easily obtained.

## HONEY CAKE.

*Ingredients.*—½ breakfast-cupful of sugar, 1 breakfast-cupful of rich sour cream, 2 breakfast-cupfuls of flour, ½ teaspoonful of carbonate of soda, honey to taste. *Mode.*—Mix the sugar and cream together; dredge in the flour, with as much honey as will flavour the mixture nicely; stir it well that all the ingredients may be thoroughly mixed; add the carbonate of soda, and beat the cake well for another 5 minutes; put it into a buttered tin, bake it from ½ to ¾ hour, and let it be eaten warm. *Time.*—½ to ¾ hour. *Average cost*, 8d. *Sufficient* for 3 or 4 persons. *Seasonable* at any time.

## HORSERADISH.

This root, scraped, is always served with hot roast beef, and is used for garnishing many kinds of boiled fish. Let the horseradish remain in cold water for an hour; wash it well, and with a sharp knife scrape it into very thin shreds, commencing from the thick end of the root. Arrange some of it lightly in a small glass dish, and the remainder use for garnishing the joint; it should be placed in tufts round the border of the dish, with 1 or 2 bunches on the meat. *Average cost*, 2d. per stick. *Seasonable* from October to June.

## HORSERADISH SAUCE, to serve with Roast Beef.

*Ingredients.*—4 tablespoonfuls of grated horseradish, 1 teaspoonful of pounded sugar, 1 teaspoonful of salt, ½ teaspoonful of pepper, 2 teaspoonfuls of made mustard; vinegar. *Mode.*—Grate the horseradish, and mix it well with the sugar, salt, pepper, and mustard; moisten it with sufficient vinegar to give it the consistency of cream, and serve in a tureen; 3 or 4 tablespoonfuls of cream added to the above very much improve the appearance and flavour of this sauce. To heat it to serve with hot roast beef, put it in a *bain marie* or a jar, which place in a saucepan of boiling water; make it hot, but do not allow it to boil, or it will curdle.

*Note.*—This sauce is a great improvement on the old-fashioned way of serving cold-scraped horseradish with hot roast beef. The mixing of the cold vinegar with the warm gravy cools and spoils everything on the plate. Of course, with cold meat, the sauce should be served cold.

## HORSERADISH VINEGAR.

*Ingredients.*—¼ lb. of scraped horseradish, 1 oz. of minced shalot, 1 drachm of cayenne, 1 quart of vinegar. *Mode.*—Put all the ingredients into a bottle, which shake well every day for a fortnight. When it is thoroughly steeped, strain and bottle, and it will be fit for use immediately. This will be found an agreeable relish to cold beef, &c. *Seasonable.*—This vinegar should be made either in October or November, as horseradish is then in its highest perfection.

## HOT SPICE (a Delicious Adjunct to Chops, Steaks, Gravies, &c.)

*Ingredients.*—3 drachms each of ginger, black pepper, and cinnamon, 7 cloves, ½ oz. mace, ¼ oz. of cayenne, 1 oz. grated nutmeg, 1½ oz. white pepper. *Mode.*—Pound the ingredients, and mix them thoroughly together, taking care that everything is well blended. Put the spice in a very dry glass bottle for use. The quantity of cayenne may be increased, should the above not be enough to suit the palate.

www.ingramcontent.com/pod-product-compliance
Lightning Source LLC
Chambersburg PA
CBHW081727100526
44591CB00016B/2526